The Magical Cookery of

I Foodini

Christopher H. Warren

ISBN: 9781088015988 (paperback)
ISBN: 9781088016046 (ebook)

Library of Congress Control Number: 2022904777

Because of the dynamic nature of the Internet, any web addresses or links contained in this book may have changed since publication and may no longer be valid. The views expressed in this work are solely those of the author and do not necessarily reflect the views of the publisher, and the publisher hereby disclaims any responsibility for them.

Conigliera Press rev. date: April 2022

*To Artemesia, and all the others who have
enchanted, inspired and confounded me*

Artemesia Rappoli
March 12, 1881–September 6, 1919

"I think it might be agreeable for the public to be made acquainted with these little secrets, which have excited great interest, and I think I cannot publish them in a more appropriate way than by placing them at the head of a book full of tricks revealed and mysteries explained. If the reader will kindly follow me... I will introduce him to my home, and act as his guide. Indeed, to spare him all trouble and fatigue, I will, in my capacity as ex-magician, enable him to make his journey and pay his visit without moving from his own armchair."

Jean-Eugène Robert-Houdin 1868

Contents

I Foodini Menu

Antipasti
Giancarlo's Tuscan Crostini 27
Ben's Prosciutto and Fig Pops 39
Elena's Gelatina and Salsa Verde 51
Bread and Extra Virgin Olive Oil 131

Primi
Frittata with Hops 6
Katrin's Pasta alla Carbonara 21
Spaghetti alla Gricia 29
Panzanella Bread Salad 36
Spaghetti with Shrimp 82
Jenn's Mac and Cheese 94
Cush-cush Gnocchi with Butter
    and Sage 104

Secondi
Risotto with Asparagus 7
Annetta's Ravioli with Ivana's Ragù 15
Polenta with Bruno's Porcini
    and Sausage Sauce 50
Baccalà- Salted Cod with Chickpeas 49
Lobster Risotto 92
Bruna's Acquacotta 38
Prosciutto-Wrapped Mahi-Mahi 106
Gianfranco and Mario's Peace
    Pizza 118
Parmigiana 124

Dolci
Ricotta with Coffee 9
Vincenzo's Gelo di Melone 58
Vincenzo's Biancomangiare 57
Gli Sfratti 69
Creme de Abacate 83
Jenn's Cacao Faux Mousse 108

Bevande
Elderflower Cordial 8
Jenn's White Wine Sangria 96

Vini
La Conigliera Rosso Toscano 42
La Gawenne Grapefruit
    Papaya Wine 72
La Gawenne Mango Passion
    Wine 72

Introduction

Foodies can be akin to sorcerers. From humble country homes to Michelin starred kitchens, there are secret recipes passed from generation to generation and tricks of the trade that can astound onlookers and delight their palates. When I observed an elderly Italian *contadina* extract 3½ kilos of three different types of cheese from 10 liters of ewe's milk, I noted in my previous cookery book that it seemed like "a genuine miracle." Equally impressive is the winemaker's art when natural yeasts are employed to initiate the fermentation of grape juice, and the bubbling cap of grape skins swells and pushes up in the wine vats. Similarly, a baker uses a "mother" – a preparation of living yeast that can be kept viable literally for centuries – to make dough rise and produce sourdough bread. At table, a simple soufflé, made just with beaten egg whites and either a sweet or savory flavor, can dazzle. In the kitchen, a chef can create a combination of ingredients that can be surprising and delicious: even just a pinch of salt can make a sweet dessert pop.

One of my favorite concoctions is a *creme de abacate* that I remember from my very early years in Salvador de Bahia. Avocado is officially a fruit, but it is generally used in savory dishes. In Brazil, where avocados are abundant, it is also mixed with sugar and cream and made into a delicious parfait. That dessert became a favorite when I was running the kitchen of the Zandoli Inn in Dominica one recent year, and the recipe is in this book. Another recipe is for pizza dough. Traditionally a wood-fired stove was used for baking bread and making pizza, and it requires considerable expertise to temper the oven properly, redolent of the dark arts. Further, a talented pizza thrower would not be out of place on a stage of prestidigitators. Trained chefs acquire a variety of show-worthy skills. The butchery of a side of beef, the dismantling of a duck, and the filleting of fish require considerable dexterity with knives. Even just the rapid slicing and dicing of an onion can be mesmerizing.

Therefore, to liken a chef to a magician is appropriate, and the title of this book refers to the great illusionist Erik Weisz. Weisz adopted the stage name Houdini in homage to the French magician Jean-Eugène Robert-Houdin. Apparently, Weisz incorrectly thought that in French, an *i* at the end of a name means "akin to" – thus Houdini-like. In Italian, an *i* at the end of a noun simply indicates that it is plural. In addition, *i* is one of the definite articles used before masculine plural nouns. So, "The Foodini" is I Foodini.

I Foodini are primarily three foodies: myself, Sean Lawson, and Jennifer Andreoli. In the over 30 years that I have lived in the medieval hilltown of Sorano in Tuscany, I have had the great fortune to be invited into the homes of and been fed by many of the welcoming townspeople. Two, in particular, became my adoptive aunties, and between them, they taught me most of what I know about the magic of the Italian table. Unlike me, both Sean and Jenn had formal training at culinary schools. Sean settled in Sorano with his Italian wife, Emma, about 15 years after I had arrived. He had previously been working in London for seven years as a chef at various restaurants. Sean was born in Sunderland, England, where his grandmother had a fish and chips shop, which inspired him eventually to follow her into the food preparation business. When he was young, his family moved to Auckland, so most of his schooling, culinary training, and first ten years of cooking jobs were in New Zealand.

Jennifer – Jenn – is originally from Toronto, where her mother and stepfather worked in the film industry. Jenn's busy parents often left her to fend for herself, so she became quite an adept and confident cook from an early age. Jenn's father, Tony Hall, was trained as an architect but was a set designer by trade. He had a dream to build a boutique hotel in the tropics, and so the family left the rat race behind and moved to the Caribbean island of Dominica when Jenn was eight. The beautiful Zandoli Inn opened in 1992, but Jenn continued to go back and forth between Canada and Dominica. She eventually got her culinary degree, earned her cooking chops, and then in 1996 opened and was the chief chef at the very successful Universal Grill restaurant in Toronto. Tony Hall died suddenly in 1998, and eventually Jenn returned permanently to Dominica to help her mother run the Zandoli Inn – and she made the restaurant the best on the island.

The motivation for the 1 Foodini project came from two seemingly unfortunate circumstances. Firstly, through no fault of my own, a noted publishing house canceled another cookbook of mine, entitled *Feasts from Paradiso*. Not long after that, a girlfriend broke up with me and apparently, as an act of contrition, decided to give me a rather extravagant gift – an iPad. It didn't take long for me to come up with the idea of using that iPad to shoot a series of videos about visiting the kitchens of my friends – some of whom were featured in the canceled book. Sean had previously helped with the preparation of the five feasts that make up that book, so including him in our subsequent culinary adventures seemed natural.

The first episode occurs in my garden, which is the setting for *Feasts from Paradiso*, and I begin by saying that the purpose of the video is to bring attention to that book in the hope of selling it to another publisher. We drive to the garden in my vintage 1989 Citroën BX sports car, which we then use to get to most of the destinations in the next nine videos.

The Dominica edition of the videos came out of a journey 1 took to the Caribbean island with that same former girlfriend. She attended a seminar in 2011 on another island, so 1 proposed meeting her afterwards. I was tempted to go to St. Lucia, as 1 lived there as a boy over four idyllic years in the late 1960s and had not returned since 1975. However, 1 got cold feet because 1 had read that development had changed the island considerably. When my family moved from St. Lucia to England in 1969, we went by a Geest banana boat and stopped off briefly in Dominica to take on more bananas before heading across the Atlantic. I had distinct memories of the sleepy capital, Roseau, and had heard that the island had been little developed in the ensuing 40 years. Although St. Lucia's population had doubled since the 1970s, Dominica's remained the same. In fact, the island is incredibly unspoiled and very beautiful. Two-thirds of the volcanic island is still covered by tropical rainforest, and half of that is protected as forest reserves. So, we ended up staying ten days and had such a wonderful time that we decided to seek out property to buy.

The following year we returned to Dominica with the idea of investing in a small eco-development and stayed our first nights back on island at the Zandoli Inn, which had been fully booked the year before. I was particularly impressed by Jenn's potent rum punches and delicious and inventive meals. I understood that Jenn did not like guests poking their noses in the kitchen, but I persisted. I impressed her enough with my cookery savvy that she invited me to help prepare dinner on our last evening there. Shortly after that, my girlfriend informed me that she no longer wanted to buy land on the island nor be involved with me anymore, and she flew off. It took me a couple of days to recover, but I soon realized it was all for the best. I rightly suspected that there were many more lovely places to discover, and I got myself a cutlass and set off into the rainforest, beginning ten years of winter adventures on the island. I did eventually find an extraordinary piece of land on a peninsula jutting out into the Atlantic, and I tell the amusing and sometimes maddening tale of trying to acquire it in a story entitled "The Pentecostal Bishop, the Catholic Cardinal, and the Rastafarian Lawyer – Proceedings in Paradise," to be published in an upcoming book.

The following year I rented a bamboo hut for about a month and kept up my friendship with Jenn, visiting the Zandoli Inn often. Toward the end of that stay, Jenn proposed that I run the kitchen the next winter – her son needed some surgery in Toronto, so she could not be at the Inn for the tourist season. I had not cooked professionally in a restaurant before, but we were both confident that I could manage, and I was pleased to get a room in exchange for the work. It was a bit of a baptism by fire and challenging, particularly as I felt that I somehow had to meet Jenn's high standards and not disappoint the expectations of guests new and old. It all went well, and I enjoyed adapting some of my European/ Italian recipes by using local ingredients. The following year, I again stayed at the Zandoli Inn, and that was when Jenn and I collaborated in the kitchen and made the Dominica-edition videos.

There is some slight irony that Italy and Dominica should be the settings for the shows, as the Italian explorer Cristoforo Colombo "discovered" Dominica on his second voyage across the Atlantic in 1493. He rather unimaginatively named it in Latin for the day of the week he spotted it on – Sunday. There continues to be a movement to reinstate the original Carib Indian name *Wai'tukukubuli*, meaning "Tall is her body."

All the videos were shot almost exclusively with the gifted iPad, which means they were not of a high quality compared to what one would get with the type of sophisticated cameras used for broadcast cooking shows. Despite the image and audio limitations, I took it as a self-imposed challenge to use the iPad, using only ambient light and sometimes affixing a cheap microphone to the tablet or, if the audio didn't come through well, just overdubbing some commentary. I then edited the videos as best I could with the iMovie app. The results are a bit rough but work well. There were no second takes, as I just filmed the uninterrupted process of preparing food with friends. The content – about places in Italy and Dominica, the people there, and their recipes – is what matters. In fact, the dodgy shots, blurred and grainy images, and muffled remarks lend verisimilitude and some charm to the stories told.

One by one, the videos were uploaded to YouTube. As we received very positive reactions to the first episodes, I sent links to some people I know in the food entertainment industry. Amanda Hesser never responded, but she obviously thought the idea was good: her fledgling cooking channel, Food52, almost immediately started presenting food preparation videos shot with an iPad. And it seems that Jamie Oliver was taken with my concept of driving to destinations in a 1980s white vintage car, as in short order, Jamie and his sidekick Jimmy were going on similar culinary road trips. The only difference from I Foodini is that everything is a bit more posh. He visited the kitchens of celebrities in his 3-liter V6 Ford Capri (my Citroën is only 1.4 liters and four cylinders), and the production values are of a TV broadcast standard. No hard feelings – I was actually quite pleased that I Foodini's humble videos could be inspirational for the muckety-mucks.

I did have proposals from producers. One insisted on bringing an "iron chef" on board, but he soon lost interest as I preferred to have Sean riding shotgun in the Citroën. Another fellow brought a little Hollywood Babylon to sleepy Sorano. His fondness for grappa resulted in some uproarious scenes in the main town piazza that will long be remembered. After two trips to the emergency room, I put him on a flight back to L.A.

Nom.com was started by one of the founders of YouTube as a live streaming food channel featuring chefs worldwide. I Foodini did four pilot videos for the San Francisco-based company. Still, there were seemingly insurmountable technical problems with streaming from out-of-the-way locations like Sorano and Dominica – although I even did one from Manhattan for them. The idea was good, but the company folded after just two years.

I Foodini persevered. We have done over 20 videos and live streams to date, and from our foodie friends have accumulated recipes, stories, tricks, and magic aplenty to fill this modest tome.

Episode 1
In the garden

Episode 1

Wine features in most of the I Foodini videos, and I first met Sean in one of the local wine bars in Sorano, where we have subsequently lifted many a glass. In fact, he has just become the proprietor of that same wine bar, La Cantina dei Sapori, where he serves delicious, simple dishes and excellent local wines. So it seemed apt to use one of Turiddu's lovely arias from Mascagni's *Cavalleria rusticana* for the opening credits of this and the subsequent Italian episodes.

Intanto amici, qua,	Meanwhile, friends, here,
Beviamone un bicchiere!	Let's have a glass!
Viva il vino spumeggiante	Long live the sparkling wine
Nel bicchiere scintillante,	In the glistening glass
Come il riso dell'amante	Like the lover's laughter.
Mite infonde il giubilo!	It inspires jubilation!
Viva il vino ch'è sincero	Long live wine that is sincere,
Che ci allieta ogni pensiero,	That gladdens our every thought,
E che annega l'umor nero,	And drowns dark moods
Nell'ebbrezza tenera.	With tender intoxication.

Sean and I introduce ourselves at a bend in the road with a
spectacular view of our hometown, Sorano, in the background. The
Citroën is parked nearby, outside Luigino Porri's pottery. We get
in the car and turn off the asphalted road onto a path that leads to
my garden. Before the main road was constructed in the 1930s, this
path was the primary route from the north, leading down into the
Lente river valley and then up to town. Hewn out of the volcanic
tufa cliffside by the Etruscans some 2,500 years ago, in places there
are high galleries so narrow that donkey-drawn carts long ago left
furrows in the walls. The Citroën barely gets through, with perhaps
a centimeter on either side. Fortunately, a typically mischievous, if
not malevolent townsperson told me that he had driven his small
Fiat Panda down that same path, so I decided to chance it with the
Citroën. As it was so tight, when I saw Enrico again, I simply told
him that I had tried to drive down the Etruscan path as he had
suggested. Assuming that I had had a misadventure, he insisted
that he had never said such a thing, nor had he driven his Panda on
the path. I continue to thank him to this day, to which he responds
with an annoyed shrug, because I have countless times taken
supplies down to my garden and caves and then produce and wood
up to my home – impossible without having made that first attempt
with the Citroën.

Once we get to my garden, we climb down the 17 steps to the first of the properties I purchased – a terrace with four Bronze-Age caves. It was Luigino, the elderly potter from up on the main road, who gave me some important and surprising history about the plot. The first of the caves had belonged to his great-uncle and was the town's oldest pottery. The other three were where Sorano's last cave inhabitant lived and worked, and she was to become one of the central figures of another of my previously published books, *All the Noise of It*. Her Tuscan nickname was La Topa, and she was the namesake for the Grotta della Topa. La Topa had been the town prostitute and had practiced the oldest profession in what is translated into English as the Pussy Cave.

I give a brief tour of what has become noted on Google Maps as Il Giardino della Topa – Pussy's Garden – while Sean readies one of the small caves where I had set up a table and an old Zoppas stove. This is where we had previously prepared many of the meals celebrated in *Feasts from Paradiso*.

On the occasion of this first I Foodini video, we invite our friends Sabine and Kath to join us for lunch. We begin with a frittata made with wild hops that I had foraged that morning. We then have a risotto with asparagus, washed down with my garden-made elderflower cordial and homemade red wine. We prepare whipped ricotta with sambuca liqueur, ground coffee, and strawberries for dessert. To end the day, we all pile into the Citroën and go for a veritable rollercoaster ride at speed, down the path, through "the jungle," as Kath exclaimed, over the river, and then up to town.

Frittata with Hops

6 servings

300 grams (11 ounces) hop shoots, chopped
1 onion, finely chopped
2 tablespoons olive oil
8 eggs
Salt and pepper

Wash the hop shoots, chop them into small pieces, and place them into a medium-sized frying pan with 100 milliliters (½ cup) of water. Add the onion, cover, and simmer for 4 minutes. Remove lid and continue to cook until the water has evaporated. Add the olive oil and fry the hops-and-onion mixture for 3 minutes or until golden. In a bowl, beat the eggs and season with salt and pepper. Stir the eggs into the hops mixture. Cover and cook on medium heat for 4 minutes. Flip the frittata onto a plate and then slide it back into the pan to cook the other side for another 2–3 minutes. Slice into individual portions and serve.

Risotto with Asparagus

6 servings

2 liters (2 quarts) broth (chicken or vegetable)
500 grams (1 pound) asparagus, trimmed,
  with the tough ends set aside for broth
2 tablespoons olive oil
1 large onion, finely chopped
600 grams (3 cups) rice, preferably riso Roma. If not,
  Carnaroli or Arborio.
150 milliliters (⅔ cup) white wine
20 grams (2 tablespoons) butter (if the rice is Carnaroli
  wor Arborio. No butter is needed if the rice is the Roma variety.)
75 grams (2½ ounces) freshly grated Parmesan cheese
Salt and pepper

Snap each asparagus spear individually into two pieces. The tops
will be used for the risotto and the woody ends for making the
broth. Bring the chicken or vegetable broth to a boil, add the
asparagus ends, and simmer for 20 minutes. Coarsely chop the
asparagus tops and put them in a pan with half a glass of water.

Bring to a boil, cover, and cook until the asparagus is just tender. Drain, and set the asparagus to one side. Put the olive oil and the onion into a wide heavy-bottomed pan and gently fry until soft. Stir in the rice so that the grains become very lightly toasted and coated with the oil. Pour in the glass of wine, stirring until absorbed. Now add a ladle of the hot broth, and turn the heat down to a simmer. While gently stirring the rice, gradually add the broth a ladle at a time until it is all absorbed. Once cooked, in about 15 minutes, the rice will be creamy and slightly firm. Remove from the heat and stir in the butter (if needed), asparagus tops, and grated Parmesan cheese. Salt and pepper to taste. Serve immediately.

Elderflower Cordial

50 elderflower umbels, freshly picked
3 lemons, sliced
1 kilo (2.2 pounds) white sugar
1 kilo (2.2 pounds) brown sugar
75 grams (6 tablespoons) citric acid
2.5 liters (2⅔ quarts) water

Choose 50 of the biggest and whitest umbels or flower clusters. Remove any insects from the umbels, but do not rinse the flowers, as much of the flavorful pollen would be washed away. Strip the small white flowers from the umbels, placing them in a large ceramic or metal bowl and removing as much of the acrid green stalks as possible. Add the halved and thinly sliced lemons to the bowl. In a pot, bring the water to a boil, and pour in the sugar and citric acid, stirring until dissolved. Immediately pour the hot water over the flowers and lemons and stir. Cover the bowl and place it in a very cool pantry or refrigerator for four days, stirring the mixture twice daily. Sieve the mixture, and strain the liquid through cheesecloth or cotton gauze. Pour the cordial into 50 centiliter (16 ounce) plastic water bottles, putting one or two in the fridge and the rest in the freezer for future use.

Diluting the cordial with about ten parts water makes a wonderfully refreshing summer drink.

Ricotta with Coffee

6 servings

500 grams (1 pound) sweet ricotta
3 tablespoons icing sugar
40 milliliters (1½ ounces) sambuca liqueur
3 teaspoons pulverized Italian roast coffee
12 strawberries, sliced into small pieces

Whisk together the ricotta, sugar, and sambuca until creamy, then place in a refrigerator for 1 hour. Apportion the ricotta onto six dessert plates, sprinkle each with a half teaspoon of coffee, and garnish with the strawberries.

Episode 2
In town
with Annetta

Episode 2

In the second episode, Sean and I drive through the narrow streets of the medieval hilltown of Sorano to my front door. We have an appointment with Annetta Forti, a neighbor who taught me much of what I know about the Italian table. However, before we join her, we stop off in my kitchen to prepare a ragù that I devised with another elderly neighbor, Ivana Castrini. As I have written elsewhere, Ivana and Annetta lived just a few doors from each other. They were friends, basically cooked the same dishes in the same way, had never eaten together, but still expressed very poor opinions of one another's cooking. They also both essentially adopted me as their American nephew and were extremely possessive of me. Annetta was happy for me to make the ragù, but she assumed that it was her recipe. In fact, it *was* her recipe, as it is the classic Sorano ragù – different from a ragù made in any other Italian town. The difference can just come down to what vegetables, like celery and carrots, are used – or none at all. Also, other towns might exclude the use of garlic. However, on one occasion, when Ivana was making a ragù, I suggested that she add some sprigs

of thyme, which grows wild and abundantly in my garden. I love thyme, but it curiously is not used as an herb for cooking in Sorano. So, Ivana agreed and was quite pleased with the result, and I have continued to make Sorano ragù with thyme from that time.

Ivana's Ragù

One medium-sized onion, finely chopped
3 cloves garlic, finely chopped
2 tablespoons olive oil, plus more for drizzling
300 grams (10 ounces) lean ground beef
200 grams (7 ounces) ground pork
500 grams (1 pound) Italian peeled tomatoes
3 sprigs fresh thyme
150 milliliters (⅔ cup) red wine
Salt and pepper to taste

Gently fry the onion and garlic in a pan with two tablespoons of olive oil until slightly golden. Turn heat up to medium, add the beef and pork, and cook until the meat browns. Add the peeled tomatoes – broken up in the pan with a wooden spoon – thyme, and wine, and simmer the ragù for 2 hours. Stir occasionally, adding water to prevent the sauce from drying out. Stir in a generous drizzle of olive oil. Add salt and pepper to taste.

We then head off down the short lane, where Annetta and I both lived, with a bottle of wine and "Annetta's" ragù. In her kitchen, Sean is sous-chef, and he and Annetta make tortelli together. Once prepared, the tortelli are cooked, placed in a large bowl, and the ragù is spooned on top. Sean's wife, Emma, joins us for lunch, and everyone agrees that the tortelli are delicious – and Annetta, seemingly not detecting the thyme, praises me for making her ragù so well.

Annetta's Ravioli with Ricotta and Spinach

6 servings

For the pasta:
500 grams (1.1 pounds) flour
4 eggs
For the ravioli filling:
100 grams (3.5 ounces) fresh spinach
500 grams (1.1 pounds) ricotta
2 pinches cinnamon
Salt to taste

Make a mound of the flour on your work surface. Form a well in the center, and crack the eggs into it. Using a fork, mix the eggs and slowly incorporate the flour until the pasta begins to bind. With floured hands, knead the pasta for up to 5 minutes, until smooth and elastic. Wrap the pasta in cellophane and place it in a refrigerator.

Steam the spinach for about 3 minutes or until tender. Drain, and once cool, squeeze dry. Finely chop the spinach, and mix in a bowl with the ricotta and cinnamon to form a paste.

Using a rolling pin on a floured work surface, roll out the pasta as thinly as possible – ideally, as Annetta does, to about a 1-millimeter thickness. Although Annetta sometimes uses a pasta machine to make ravioli, you want to end up with strips about 90 centimeters (35 inches) long and 11 centimeters (4¼ inches) wide. Evenly place 11 heaped teaspoons of the ricotta mixture along each strip of pasta. Fold the strips over the filling, and cut between each mound of ricotta to form the individual ravioli. With the tines of a fork, seal the three open edges.

Allow 6 to 8 ravioli per person, and any ravioli left over can be wrapped in cellophane and frozen for future use. Put a large pot of salted water to boil. Cook the ravioli for 3 to 4 minutes. Drain and serve with the ragù.

Episode 3

Carbonara with Katrin

Episode 3

We stay close to home when we visit Katrin Melcher and Martin Ostertag. Katrin's mother, Lella Gallino, is originally from Genoa, and her father, Willy, was from Hamburg, Germany. They and I were some of the original *forestieri* – outsiders – to buy homes in Sorano. In the introduction to the episode, I note that when I first came to the town in the 1980s, there were only about 100 year-round residents, down from some 4,000 before the Second World War. Thanks to the outsiders who came from various Italian cities and far-flung places like Scandinavia, England, the United States, Australia, New Zealand, Japan, and Uruguay, the town was saved from almost total abandonment.

Willy was the first violinist of the Melos Quartet, one of the premier string quartets of the latter half of the 20th century. Like her father Willy, Katrin is a violinist and plays with the Southwest German Radio Symphony Orchestra. She also plays as a chamber music performer, and has recorded pieces as a violist. Katrin's husband recently retired as the first cellist of the same Freiburg-based orchestra but continues as an internationally recognized recording artist and highly sought-after teacher.

Katrin and Martin bought and renovated a home in Sorano. I have often been invited for suppers and morning coffee, as Katrin has a very good Saeco cappuccino machine. Katrin learned about Italian cooking very ably from her Northern Italian mother but gives a classic Central Italian dish a Germanic touch. Both Sean and I have to admit that adding a shot glass of milk to the standard egg and pancetta bacon mix makes Katrin's carbonara likely the best we have ever had.

(Left) The view of the Lente river from Katrin's window

(Above) Katrin has a lovely collection of art- including one of my sculptures- *a reclining lady.*

Katrin's Pasta Alla Carbonara

4 servings

5 slices cured pancetta
1 garlic clove, finely chopped
2 tablespoons olive oil
5 eggs (4 whole eggs and 1 yolk)
1 cup Parmesan cheese
2 tablespoons milk
Pepper to taste
500 grams (1 pound) spaghetti

Chop up the pancetta. Put the olive oil in a large pan and fry the pancetta and garlic until golden.

Break the four eggs (one for each person) into a bowl, add the additional yolk, Parmesan, milk, and seasoning, and whisk together.

Cook the spaghetti in boiling salted water until *al dente*. Drain the spaghetti and pour it into the bowl with the egg mixture. Add the pancetta from the pan without the fat. Mix and serve.

Episode 4 & 5

Classic Tuscan &
Roman Dishes
with Giancarlo

Episodes 4 and 5

Monte Elmo rises north of Sorano to a modest elevation of about 850 meters, and a curious local legend is associated with it. It is claimed that a magnetic lode within the mount has attracted the odd assortment of outsiders that have descended upon Sorano and the surrounding area. In Italian, a magnet is a *calamita*, so those drawn to Sorano are called the *calamitati*. One of the first of the calamitati was Giancarlo Cortesi. He bought his home in 1979 in the town of Elmo, which is on the flanks of the Monte, about six kilometers from Sorano. I have enjoyed many excellent meals in Elmo, as Giancarlo is an expert cook, although he is a celebrated actor by profession.

Giancarlo is Roman and was born in the city's center at Piazza di Sant'Eustachio. It is just around the corner from the Pantheon, but one of the reasons that I am so familiar with his birthplace is because of the piazza's famous eponymous bar. Katrin's cappuccino is very good in Sorano. Still, the version at Sant'Eustachio il Caffè is sublime, and the secret of its silky creaminess is so guarded that it is prepared behind a screen – trickery worthy of another I Foodini exposé.

The first recipe that Giancarlo prepares for us in his kitchen is a classic from the Eternal City – Spaghetti alla Gricia – and this is the subject of episode 5. The elements are simple: cured pig cheeks, pecorino romano cheese, and black pepper. The brilliance of the dish comes from the quality and exact measures of the ingredients – and the way he makes it. Giancarlo made an interesting discovery in 2007 when he was on tour with his show of four comic monologues adapted from the stories of Massimo Bontempelli. While performing at the Grazia Deledda theatre in Paulilatino, Sardinia, he stopped by a local cheese factory. He was surprised to find, in addition to the Sardinian pecorino sardo, also pecorino romano cheese for sale. Made from sheep's milk, pecorino romano is one of Italy's oldest cheeses and was a staple food for the legionnaires of Ancient Rome. It is also an essential ingredient for many of Rome's most iconic dishes, like carbonara and *cacio e pepe*. Although it was made originally in Rome's region of Latium, most of the production has now shifted to the island of Sardinia, with its wide-open spaces and large sheep population.

From when he was a small boy until he left home to pursue his career as an actor, Giancarlo would spend the summers with his mother's sister at her farmhouse near Montecatini Terme in Tuscany. His aunt's husband was a *mezzadro*, a sharecropper, which

meant that a wealthy landowner owned his home and all the land
he farmed. Half of what Giancarlo's uncle produced went to the
owner, but the family lived well despite that. Giancarlo's happiest
memories were of helping his uncle in the vineyard and garden
and his aunt in her kitchen. The second recipe, and the subject of
episode 4, that Giancarlo prepares are the Tuscan crostini that his
aunt would make at the celebratory time of the *trebbiatura* in July,
when local families would gather to help with the threshing of the
wheat grain for making flour. While making the crostini topping,
Giancarlo remarks that he must return to London, where he lived
and performed for a time, to refresh his English. Sean notes that it
is the Queen's Diamond Jubilee – 60 years on the throne – and we
all toast to her long-continued reign. I ask Giancarlo what he makes
of the Queen, and he pauses and then begins to sing the Beatles'
"Her Majesty" from the *Abbey Road* album, which was released
when he was in London. The three of us go to one of the local bars
in Sorano to share two large platters of the crostini at cocktail hour.
The crostini are quickly consumed, and the episode ends with Paul
McCartney singing "Her Majesty's a pretty nice girl..."

Giancarlo's Tuscan Crostini

1 small onion
1 shallot
300 grams (11 ounces) minced chicken liver, heart, and a very small piece of
   calf's spleen
100 grams (4 ounces) minced lean ground beef
80 milliliters (2¼ tablespoons) olive oil
100 milliliters (½ cup) white wine
3 tablespoons vinegar
3 anchovies
500 milliliters (2 cups) chicken broth
1 tablespoon tomato paste
40 grams (1½ ounces) rinsed and pressed capers
pepper to taste

As Giancarlo's aunt lived on a farm, had a variety of animals
and vegetables at hand, and had more time to devote to food
preparation, her recipe would have had a somewhat different
array of ingredients. She used rabbit liver instead of chicken liver,
which has a stronger flavor, and all of the other interior organs of a
chicken, including the gizzard and the intestines. Just cleaning the
intestines was an arduous task. She also made fresh chicken broth.
For this recipe, Giancarlo uses chicken stock powder. He might
have used a large onion but had only a small one available, so he
supplements it with a shallot.

He begins by roughly chopping the onion and shallot. He passes the
chicken liver and heart and calf's spleen through a manual mincer
together with the onion and shallot so that those ingredients are all
thoroughly mixed. He then passes the beef through the mincer.

Those minced ingredients are placed in a large pan with the olive
oil on moderate heat. The white wine, vinegar and anchovies are
then mixed in.

To 100 milliliters (½ cup) of the heated chicken broth, he mixes in a heaping tablespoon of tomato paste, which is then added to the pan. As the mixture cooks down, he slowly ladles in the rest of the broth. He then rinses the salted capers and squeezes them dry before chopping them with his curved two-handled mezzaluna (half-moon) blade. The caper mash is slid into the mix, along with a generous amount of pepper, and all continues to cook on low heat. Once a wooden spoon can be passed through the moist mixture, exposing the bottom of the pan, and liquid does not immediately fill the cleared space, it is done.

Giancarlo's aunt would have used sliced day-old stale Tuscan white bread for the crostini, but Giancarlo lightly toasts the fresh bread he has. He explains that if he had more broth, he would have done like his aunt and briefly dipped the bread in the broth – for yet more added flavor – before laying the slices on the platter and covering them with the sauce.

Spaghetti Alla Gricia

2 servings

3 slices guanciale (cured pork cheek)
250 grams (8 ounces) spaghetti or bucatini
1 cup pecorino romano
black pepper

Put a large pot of salted water on to boil. Cut the slices of guanciale lengthwise into strips, and then slice again into small cubes. Fry the guanciale in a large pan until the fat is translucent and the meat very lightly browned. Drop the spaghetti or bucatini into the pot and boil until it is almost fully cooked. Mix in three teaspoons of the pasta water with the guanciale, and then toss the pasta into the pan to finish cooking. Add the grated pecorino cheese, and mix. The cheese should have a creamy consistency, and so might need a few more tablespoons of the pasta water if it is dry. Grind some pepper to taste on top and serve.

Episode 6

La Costa d'Argento
with Bruna & Ben

Episode 6

When I was initially working on *Feasts from Paradiso*, I went to one of the more talked-about and highly reviewed Italian restaurants in Manhattan. To get a sense of the quality of the basic ingredients used, I ordered an antipasto of bresaola (cured beef) on a bed of arugula, drizzled with olive oil. Those three ingredients should have very distinct flavors. The dish was insipid. The rest of the meal was mediocre. As I was leaving, the chef was sitting at the bar and being kowtowed to by two well-known celebrities. There is no accounting for taste, but it may be that Italians are more discriminating about food because they are accustomed to local, fresh, and flavorful produce. What I ate in that Manhattan eatery would have been sent back in a top restaurant in Italy.

Italian recipes and descriptions of food preparation in Italy tend to be quite simple and certainly rely upon the best ingredients. In this episode, Sean and I initially drive 70 kilometers to the seaside town of Orbetello to meet with Bruna Savelli. She and Sean prepare two typical Tuscan poor-man's dishes in her kitchen: an onion soup called *cipollata* and a *panzanella* bread salad. Orbetello lies on a lagoon that was formed between two isthmuses. Over two millennia, they were transformed into broad causeways with long beaches named Feniglia and Giannella that connect the mainland to the island of Monte Argentario. We carry on driving another 20 kilometers to the far side of the island to meet my friend Benedetto "Ben" Pignatti Morano at his lovely villa at Le Canelle. There Ben instructs us on the proprieties of fine prosciutto consumption. We go for a swim and then head back to Sorano, where we meet up again with Bruna and her son Nicola Santoro at his restaurant, the Cantina L'Ottava Rima.

We were late for our meeting with Giancarlo in the previous episode, so I put the Citroën through its paces on the very windy road to Elmo. Discerning viewers subsequently advised me that the sounds of double-clutching, heel-to-toe shifting, squealing tires, the straining engine, and Sean's flattering exclamations that my driving was like that of the great grand prix driver Stirling Moss did not make a very good soundtrack. So, on this much longer journey to the coast, I popped into the cassette deck a mixed tape I made in the late 80s – songs that came out around the time I first came to Sorano and when the Citroën was constructed. While driving, when I'm not talking about the history of Orbetello or the friends we are to visit, we are accompanied by the likes of Grandmaster Flash, Public Enemy, Crystal Waters, EMF, George Michael, and the Red Hot Chili Peppers.

(Above) Entering Orbetello

Bruna was born in Orbetello to Tobia Savelli and Antonietta Papini – who were both from Sorano. At that time, Tobia was an illiterate itinerant worker who would travel from Sorano down to the fertile plains of the Maremma around Orbetello during the harvest season. He was self-taught and became an activist for the rural peasantry that had no rights and worked for the wealthy landowners under difficult and sometimes abusive conditions in what was still essentially a feudal society. Tobia settled in Orbetello with Antonietta and, through extraordinary force of character, became the mayor of Orbetello. He was one of the most important proponents for agrarian reform, which after the Second World War resulted in many lands being seized from the wealthy and redistributed to the peasants. Giancarlo's sharecropper uncle in Montecatini Terme would also have benefited from this type of government program – he became the owner of his portion of the farmhouse and the land he farmed.

Bruna learned the recipes of Sorano from her mother, but also those of Orbetello and the lagoon where bottarga cured fish roe is famously produced, for instance, and became a formidable cook in her own right. Bruna's son, Nicola, decided around 2000 to return to his roots in Sorano, take over and renovate an old wine cantina that had belonged to his grandparents, and open the restaurant. Bruna is often the chef and advises him on the menu. Still, Nicola has very strong ideas of his own and excludes typical restaurant fare like fried potatoes, spaghetti with tomato sauce, and *fiorentina* beef steaks. He demands that all the food and wine be local, the recipes original, and he has created a very special wine tavern.

Benedetto and I were studying in graduate school at New York University at the same time – he business and I anthropology – but we didn't know each other then. Shortly after I came to Italy, I met him through a mutual friend. We soon determined that we were born only seven days apart and have been very good friends for over 30 years. Ben is a businessman, real-estate developer, and accomplished watercolorist. In addition to his villa on the

(Left) Bruna and Nicola at the Ottava Rima

very exclusive Monte Argentario, he also bought a warehouse in the Trastevere neighborhood of Rome at an advantageous time and made a fabulous home out of it. Ben comes from the landed gentry class that Tobia Savelli inveighed against, and although he does not ever talk about it, the busts and portraits that decorate his properties hint at some type of nobility. He once showed me a photograph of the impressive Ducal Palace in Modena and indicated that until recently, it had belonged to his family. Modena is in an area renowned for Parmesan cheese and prosciutto. Ben has a private source for his prosciutto, which is of a quality that you would probably never get – not even in Manhattan.

Panzanella Bread Salad

2 servings

½ red pepper
Celery heart
2 tomatoes
½ cucumber, peeled
½ red onion
¼ kilo (8 ounces) of stale Tuscan
   bread

3 tablespoons extra virgin olive oil
1 teaspoon vinegar
salt to taste
sprinkle of pepper
balsamic vinegar

This meal is about as simple as it gets and was commonly eaten for lunch when the farmers worked in the fields. Slice up the vegetables and put them in a medium-sized bowl. Take roughly a quarter of a loaf of stale Tuscan bread – made without salt, it becomes stale after just a day or two. As Bruna says, the farmers from Sorano would rinse whatever vegetables they may have had and then also soaked the stale bread in the clear running water of the Lente river, which is in the valley below the town. Bruna recreates the tradition by running the bread under her kitchen tap. Once wet, she squeezes the bread partly dry and then breaks the bread up into very small pieces. The bread is mixed with the vegetables, olive oil, vinegar, salt, and pepper. The salad is served with a drizzle of balsamic vinegar.

Bruna's Acquacotta

6 servings

2 celery stalks
2 leeks
5 large onions – red, yellow, and white
3 shallots
6 tablespoons extra virgin olive oil
150 milliliters (⅔ cup) white wine
400 grams (1 pound) canned, peeled Italian tomatoes
Sliced and toasted Tuscan bread or croutons (optional)
6 eggs

Acquacotta sounds decidedly unappealing, as it means "cooked water" in Italian. But it is more like an onion soup, thus its other name – *cipollata*. Roughly slice and chop up the celery stalks, leeks, onions, and shallots. Place them in a pan with the olive oil and let the vegetables sweat down until they are soft. Pour in the glass of wine and cook until the wine has been absorbed. Add the tomatoes and simmer on low heat for a couple of hours, checking occasionally to make sure it does not dry out, adding a little water if necessary. When it is ready to be served, the eggs can be dropped into the hot soup until cooked. I prefer to poach the eggs in boiling water for three minutes so that they are a perfect consistency for the dish – with the egg whites thoroughly cooked and the yolk runny. Some people like to place a slice of toasted Tuscan bread, scraped with a clove of garlic, at the bottom of the soup bowl, and others serve it with croutons. Bruna presents her delicious version with bread and a drizzle of olive oil.

Ben's Prosciutto and Fig Pops

4 servings

8 slices prosciutto
8 fresh ripe peeled figs
Modena balsamic vinegar

Using the most exclusive Parma prosciutto and Modena balsamic
vinegar, these prosciutto-wrapped figs can be a rarefied treat. But
even with more readily available ham, they are quite delicious.
Ideally, each serving is popped into your mouth whole, so, as
Ben says, when you bite into them, there is an explosion of the
wonderful complementary flavors. In the video, Ben instructs those
who have a leg of prosciutto that it should be cold, as it makes
it easier to slice it as finely as he insists. The best time to eat it is
immediately after it has been sliced, so perhaps only half of it gets
to the serving plate. Electric meat slicers generally cut from 0 to 15
millimeters, and Ben slices at .5 – paper-thin.

Citroën

I was fascinated with Citroën cars and their hydropneumatic
suspension when I was a child. Upon ignition, the cars magically
rise from a squat position, practically touching the ground, up to
the driving height. Thanks to the automatic leveling system, they
can take corners at great speed. The variable ground clearance
means that the cars can travel quickly on bumpy road surfaces,
and the chassis can be lifted further to drive on particularly rough
terrain. The futuristic Citroën DS was designed by the Italian
Flaminio Bertoni. Roland Barthes said it looked like it had "fallen
from the sky." It was known as the Goddess (*Déesse*) in France and
in Italy as *lo Squalo* – the Shark. The later-model BX was produced
in the 1980s and was quite a popular car in Europe. When I came
to Sorano, a few were driving around and rekindled my boyhood
fantasy of eventually acquiring such a Citroën. I particularly

coveted a white 1988 sports model, so when I heard that the owner was willing to sell for a very reasonable price, I gladly scrapped my clunky DAF/Volvo 66 and achieved my modest dream.

I enjoyed driving the car immensely, but I was also amused by the fact that I, for at least a couple of years, constantly had headlights flashed at me by vehicles being driven in the opposite direction, invariably by women – and there was a great assortment of them. The previous owner was quite the ladies' man. Certainly, the *topa*, the guardian spirit of my garden I wrote about in the first episode, would have approved of this detail. I have driven the car to England and back several times and as far east as Prague. But it also has uniquely permitted me to drive for 20 years down the Etruscan path to the garden. It has been a real workhorse, and I have used it to bring building materials to the garden and caves and take away produce and wood that I would never have been able to move otherwise. It could be said that I might not have renovated the caves and gardens or written my previous two books without the Citroën. Indeed, this magical car has a significant role also in the I Foodini series and this book, so it fully deserves its two pages in tribute.

Episode 7

La Vendemmia
e la Svinatura

The grape harvest and the feast of the new wine

Episode 7

The subject of this episode is the Festa della Svinatura, a celebration of the new wine. When I first settled in Sorano, there were several mostly elderly men who continued to work in a dozen or so cantinas, or wine cellars, and I initially learned how to make wine by helping some of them make theirs. Although I kept the tradition going for 25 years, nowadays there are just two cantinas still in use in the old town. One hundred years ago, most of the approximately 300 cantinas would have been producing wine, and the svinatura was a heady time. The delightfully pungent aroma of grapes fermenting in vats would have thoroughly permeated the town, and the streets literally ran with wine.

I essentially was a member of a winemaking cooperative for 20 years. During the year, I would occasionally assist Alfio in his vineyard and so was involved in each phase of growing the grapes.

Every autumn, I would harvest my grapes from the same part of the vineyard. One year there was a terribly damaging hailstorm just before the harvest, and the following year a fire swept through the vineyard, so I had to seek grapes elsewhere. That is how I got to know Roberto Tiberi, who very kindly let me select the best-looking bunches of grapes here and there around his far vaster 75-acre vineyard. Over the few years that I continued to go to Roberto, I also experimented with the percentages of the different types of grapes that went into my wine. My ideal blend became about 70 percent red ciliegiolo, 10 percent red merlot, and 20 percent white trebbiano.

The video begins with the grape harvest at Roberto's farm, Le Chiuse. Sabine, William, Roberto and I harvest the grapes over several hours, and then I load the crates into the back of the workhorse Citroën and make two trips back to the old town.

Ross and William help carry the grapes through my house and into the cul-de-sac where my cantina is. We prepare the grapes by gently crushing them before emptying them into the two large wooden vats. Like the ancients, Sabine, Ashlei, and I thoroughly tread the grapes with our bare feet. After three days, the juice begins to ferment, and the cap of skins and stems rises to the surface, which

Ross and William arrive to assist with the crushing of the grapes

Pushing down the rising cap of grape skins

Knocking the spigot into the base of the vat

necessitates pressing it to the bottom of the vat twice a day, every day for about a week. The cap is then tamped down, the vat is loosely covered, and the fermentation continues for another few days.

The day of the svinatura is when the open vats are emptied of the must juice that has fermented for ten days to two weeks. Barrels and demijohns are partially filled with the new free-run wine. Sean comes to help with the pressing of the remaining skins, and that resulting liquid is used to top up the various containers. It is long, quite tiring, and thirsty work. Naturally, one tends to quench one's thirst with what is available in a cantina, so by the end of the day, the winemakers might not be the fittest of cooks. Therefore the Festa della Svinatura at my home becomes almost a potluck dinner to which friends bring dishes they have made in their own kitchens and collaborate on other recipes in mine.

Baccalà, or salt cod, is standard fare for a svinatura, whether stewed, baked, or roasted. I particularly like roasting it over coals in my fireplace and serve it with black chickpeas. These *ceci neri* are unique to Italy, and a local farmer in Sorano grows them. They have a lovely nutty flavor, are more textured, and don't fall apart like the standard lighter-colored variety – and go very well with the fish. Much of the preparation is in the long soaking of both the fish and the chickpeas, so I was able to do that in advance. Sean's wife, Emma, sets to stirring the pot of cornmeal polenta while Bruno, a Sardinian entrepreneur, reheats the porcini mushroom and sausage sauce he had made previously. Elena then arrives with the gelatina.

During my early days in Sorano, there were four ladies who gathered at the beginning of my short lane and regarded me with considerable distrust. We all eventually became great friends. Annetta and Ivana have previously been described, Peppa was the wife of Luigino, the potter mentioned in the first episode, and Elena also was a very nearby neighbor.

Elena, her husband Augusto Gubernari, and their three sons left after only a couple of years as they moved up to the modern new town – as most townspeople had before them. In that relatively short time, I discovered that she is an excellent seamstress, who continues to mend my trousers, and like the other ladies, an exceptional cook.

Elena's youngest son, Leonardo, is the proprietor of one of the two butcher shops in Sorano. His pork products come from the local *salumificio*, a small artisanal meat processing facility. Many of my guests from around the world have said that the sausages bought from Leonardo are the best they have ever had. The chief butcher at the salumificio lent me his rather ancient manual sausage-stuffing apparatus so that I could make sausages for another svinatura one year. I used ground pork and ground turkey and sage to make a British Lincolnshire-type sausage for the stuffing. The butcher ironically said that my sausage was the best he had ever eaten – so new tastes can often be pleasingly surprising.

As her son runs the local butcher shop, Elena has access to all the offcuts that go into a gelatina. As any Italian butcher or local farmer who grows their own pigs will say, no part of the pig – aside from its toenails – goes to waste.

We all gather about the table and enjoy the gelatina and other dishes – all washed down with wine old and new!

Baccalà – Salted Cod with Chickpeas

6–8 servings

1 kilo (2 pounds) salted cod
500 grams (1 pound) black
   chickpeas
2 bay leaves
2 large ripe tomatoes

Salt and pepper
Extra virgin olive oil
White wine vinegar
3 tablespoons fennel flowers
   (or half the amount of crushed
   fennel seeds)

Wash the salt from the cod. Leave the fish to soak in water either
in the kitchen sink or in a large bowl for at least 24 hours, changing
the water three or four times. Separately soak the chickpeas
overnight. Drain the chickpeas. Rinse, then place in a large pot with
the bay leaves and cover with double the volume of cold water.
Bring to a boil and simmer for 2 hours, or until tender. Occasionally
skim the surface of the water to remove any foam that forms. Pour
the chickpeas into a colander and set them aside. Peel and finely
chop the tomatoes and mix with the warm chickpeas. Season with a
bit of salt and pepper, two tablespoons of olive oil, and a few drops
of vinegar. Cut the cod into six portions. Place on an oiled baking
tray and sprinkle with the fennel flowers, freshly ground pepper,
and olive oil. No salt is needed. Roast for 15 minutes in a 175
degrees C/350 degrees F oven. Divide the warm chickpea mixture
between six plates and arrange a portion of cod on top of each. Pour
a generous amount of extra virgin olive oil over each dish and serve.

Polenta with Bruno's Porcini and Sausage Sauce

6–8 servings

10 spicy Italian sausages

3 garlic cloves, sliced

2 chopped peperoncini chili peppers

2 tablespoons olive oil

1 kilo (2.2 pounds) porcini
  mushrooms

2 bay leaves

200 milliliters (7 ounces) white wine

200 milliliters (7 ounces) meat broth

1 handful of parsley

4 liters (1 gallon) salted water

1 kilo (2.2 pounds) "bramata"
  polenta (coarsely ground
  cornmeal)

Parmesan cheese

Salt and pepper

Skin the sausages and break them up into small pieces. Lightly fry the sliced garlic, chili peppers, and sausage in the olive oil until the sausage is browned and cooked through. Coarsely chop the mushrooms into bite-sized pieces and add to the pan. Simmer for 10 minutes. Toss in the bay leaves, pour in the white wine, and cook until absorbed. Add the hot meat broth and cook for another 15 minutes. Season with salt and pepper and put the sauce to one side. In a large heavy-bottomed pot, bring the salted water to boil. While vigorously stirring with a wooden spoon, pour in the polenta very slowly. After the gruel has come to boil, reduce the heat to simmer and continue to stir until the polenta has thickened – about 40 minutes. Pour the polenta out onto a large wooden cutting board, forming a disk about two centimeters (¾ inch) thick, and allow to set for about 5 minutes. Cut the polenta into slices using a palette knife. Reheat the porcini mushroom sauce. Arrange two or three slices of polenta on each plate and spoon over the sauce, topped with some freshly ground Parmesan cheese.

Elena's Gelatina and Salsa Verde (Green Sauce)

For the Gelatina:
4 pig's trotters
700 grams (1.5 pounds) pigskin
1 tablespoon salt
2 basil leaves
1 tablespoon crushed chili flakes
60 milliliters (4 tablespoons)
  white wine vinegar

For the salsa verde:
3 handfuls of parsley
1 garlic clove
1 peperoncino chili pepper
1 small jar of pickled capers
1 handful of pickled vegetables
½ tube of anchovy paste
2 tablespoons vinegar
60 milliliters (4 tablespoons) olive oil

Begin by washing the trotters and skin four or five times with hot water. Once cleaned, place them in a large pot and cover with cold water. Add the salt and the basil leaves, bring the water to a boil, and simmer for 4 hours. Lift the meat and skin out of the pot with a large slotted spoon. Remove the bones and thoroughly chop. Put the meat back in the pot with the vinegar and the chili flakes and simmer for another half hour. Pour the meat and liquid into a large Pyrex or ceramic casserole dish and let cool.

For the salsa verde, finely chop the parsley, garlic, and peperoncino and put in a medium-sized bowl. Mince the capers and vegetables, and add to the bowl with the anchovy paste, vinegar, and oil. Thoroughly mix all the ingredients.

Once the gelatin has formed in the casserole dish, spoon the salsa verde on the top and serve.

Elena Pomponi and her son Leonardo Gubernari

Episode 8

Bianco Mangiare and Gelo di Mellone with Vincenzo

Episode 8

Just as wine caves were abandoned, so were houses in Sorano, particularly after the Second World War. In its heyday, as many as 4,000 people were living in old Sorano. Today there are only about 50 year-round residents, but increasing numbers of *forestieri*, outsiders like myself, have come in and basically saved the town. Beatrice Bandarin, a painter from Rome, came in the mid-1970s to teach art in the local high school. A ceramicist boyfriend of hers settled in the early 80s. He started an art school in the Orsini fortress that attracted people from all over Italy and the world, some of whom also bought places in town. Another friend of Beatrice, Josette Molho, originally from France and married for a time to a Roman, taught jewelry making in the art school. One of her students was Orietta from Palermo, Sicily, who subsequently brought her cousin Vincenzo to visit. He says that they right away felt the strong magnetic attraction of Sorano and soon bought an apartment in 2012 – two of the latest *calamitati*.

Vincenzo was born in Camporeale, 45 kilometers from Palermo. He came from a *famiglia benestante* – a family so well off that he refers to his grandfather's lands as a *feudo* – a fiefdom of 200 *salme*, or about 800 acres. The family land used to be considerably more extensive, but it has been increasingly divided up among the heirs over the generations, and Vincenzo has passed his allotment on to his nephews. Vincenzo was the director of the chamber of commerce in Palermo and just happened to have taken early retirement when he first visited Sorano.

I have had many an excellent meal with Vincenzo, but on the occasion of our visit for this episode, he prepares two quite famous Sicilian desserts: *biancomangiare*, an almond milk pudding with Middle Eastern origins, and *gelo di melone*, a cool, refreshing jellied watermelon pudding that is very popular during the hot summers in Palermo.

(Bottom right) View from Vincenzo's apt towards Donatella's garden

Sean and I walk to Vincenzo's apartment from my place, which is
a short distance away. We admire the view from his window that
so captivated Vincenzo on his first stay, of the river valley to the
north and, to the west, a portion of the town where a medieval
tower stands above the Medici entrance to the old town. On top
of that tower, Donatella, another Roman transplant, cultivates
her small, charming garden. After making the desserts, we keep
the biancomangiare for a meal that evening and take the gelo di
melone to share with some of the neighborhood kids at Donatella's
garden. Two are the great-grandchildren of Luigino the potter
and his wife Peppa, both mentioned in the previous chapter. Their
grandchild inherited their apartment and comes to Sorano with

her family for the August holidays. The other children are the nieces of Katrin, who prepares the carbonara pasta in episode 2. Her brother, Philip Melcher, is a cellist for the symphony orchestra in Granada, and his German wife, Christina, is the first oboe player for the Royal Philharmonic of Galicia in Santiago de Compostela – both in Spain but at a distance of over 1,000 kilometers from each other. They reunite with their three girls for summer in Sorano in the apartment they bought from Elena Pomponi, who made the gelatina also in the previous episode.

Ulisse says that the gelo was 100% good.

Vincenzo's Biancomangiare

6–8 servings

1½ liters (1½ quarts) almond milk
1 liter (1 quart) whole cow's milk
500 grams (1 pound) sugar
250 grams (½ pound) cornstarch
4 teaspoons vanilla extract
3 sliced pieces of lemon rind
80 grams (6 tablespoons) blanched and lightly toasted chopped almonds
30 grams (2 tablespoons) raw chopped pistachios

Vincenzo begins by demonstrating how to make almond milk from ground almonds. The night before, he had put 250 grams (8 ounces) of the almond flour into a large bowl and poured over it 1½ liters (1½ quarts) of boiling water. That was left to rest overnight. He spoons the dense milk through a sieve and then squeezes the remaining solid through a cheesecloth to extract as much liquid as possible. It is easier and less expensive to buy almond milk in a carton, but the freshly made milk can make the difference between a good and a great result. To the 1½ liters (1½ quarts) of almond milk, he adds 1 liter (1 quart) of whole cream cow's milk. Stirred into the milk are the sugar, cornstarch, vanilla extract, and pieces of lemon rind (to be removed later). The heavy-bottomed pot is brought to a boil, and then he lets it simmer, constantly stirring it with a wooden spoon. Once the milk begins to jell, after about 15

minutes, he mixes in 50 grams (1½ ounces) of the chopped almonds and then pours the pudding into a 23 centimeter (9 inch) round ceramic pie dish. He sprinkles the remaining almonds and the pistachios on top of the biancomangiare. Vincenzo concludes by saying that if we were in Sicily, he would have gone out in the early morning and gathered a few fresh, lovely, and perfumed Sicilian jasmine flowers to add to the top of both desserts.

Vincenzo's Gelo Di Melone

6–8 servings

1½ liters (1.6 quarts) watermelon
   juice
150 grams (5 ounces) cornstarch
300–350 grams (10–12 ounces)
   sugar (depending on the sweetness
   of the watermelon)

A good pinch of cinnamon powder
3 teaspoons vanilla extract
A handful of chopped raw
   pistachios for garnish
50 grams (1¾ ounces) of good-
   quality 70 percent chocolate,
   chopped

Vincenzo begins by hollowing out a medium-sized watermelon and putting the broken-up, dark-pink flesh in a large bowl. As watermelon is about 90 percent liquid, one would need a 2–2.5 kilo (4½–5½ pounds) watermelon. He passes the flesh through a hand-cranked vegetable mill to remove the seeds. The juice is poured through a fine sieve to remove any fibrous material and then into a heavy-bottomed cooking pot. He stirs in the cornstarch and then the sugar, initially adding 300 grams (10 ounces) of sugar and then tasting the liquid. If the watermelon juice is not particularly sweet, he will adjust with more sugar. Next comes a good pinch of cinnamon – enough, he says, for a hint of cinnamon but not enough to mask the other delicate flavors. Lastly, he adds three teaspoons of vanilla extract. He sets the pot on the stove and brings the liquid to a boil, stirring constantly. Upon boiling, the liquid becomes viscous within seconds. The pot is removed from the heat, and the thickening gelo is poured and spooned into a 20 centimeter (8 inch) round ceramic pie dish. The gelo is garnished with another hint of cinnamon powder, the chopped pistachios, and the chocolate pieces representing watermelon seeds.

Episode 9

Sfratti
with Mario

Episode 9

At the beginning of this episode, I am seated outside Bar Lupi, located on the main square of Sorano, the Piazza del Municipio. A cat joins me for the introduction. She is the first of the piazza cats I came to know and is very likely the grandmother to most of the others. Thus her name became Nonna – Granny. I have taken it upon myself to care for and sterilize all her progeny. In campaigning for their better treatment, I named them after storekeepers, baristas, bartenders, bank clerks, and officials in the town hall.

Mario Lupi is from Sorano and trained as a pastry chef in the well-known town of Orvieto in Umbria, a region adjacent to Tuscany and just 45 minutes by car from Sorano. He met his wife Nadia there, and they returned to Sorano and took over his father's small bar in the center of the old town. In 1980 Mario moved up to the much larger bar in the main square, built in the 19th century, and expanded his production. One of his most popular pastries likely originated in Sorano and was taught to him by Ginevra, his sister's mother-in-law, who lived only a few doors away.

The *sfratto* is a delicious honey-and-walnut roll, which Mario markets as a Christmas treat. The true history of the dessert is betrayed by its name, which means "eviction" in Italian. There was a sizeable Jewish population in Sorano and the neighboring town of Pitigliano – to the extent that it is popularly known as "Little Jerusalem." Both towns have synagogues and ghettos. There were times when Jews were welcome, and other times not. Under Cosimo II de' Medici, Jews were evicted from their homes, and the verb for that is *sfrattare*. Authorities hammered on doors with small wooden clubs, called *sfratti*, to announce eviction. In Sorano's ghetto, there was a Jewish baker, and it is thought that he made the first sfratto in the form of the eviction club as a sweet reminder of a dark time.

Once Mario has finished demonstrating how to make sfratti, we are joined by our friend Antonio Bizzi. Mario and Antonio were, in their youth, celebrated defenders for the Sorano soccer team that, while they played, won three championships and several tournaments. Antonio also owned a wine cave directly opposite my front door, and his brother Carlo was my adoptive uncle. Carlo made wine in the cantina until his untimely death in 2008 and taught me much about the craft. Both Carlo and I benefited from Antonio's expertise, as he had left Sorano in the 1970s to make wine professionally for some big producers in Umbria and Tuscany.

(Top right) Mario proudly shows the robust spoon that his father made him after he had broken all his other store bought ones while stirring the dense filling for the sfratti

Antonio's cantina is at the beginning of the Via del Ghetto, and so it seems an appropriate place to go sample some sfratti accompanied with Antonio's excellent white wine. The three of us walk from the bar and soon enter the old town by passing under a medieval archway, the Arco dei Ferrini. Protean Mario also happens to be Sorano's poet laureate, and one of his short poems, "Ferrini's Archway," is there on a ceramic plaque.

L'arco Dei Ferrini

Mitico arco che inviti le genti
Nel borgo dove il tempo s'è fermato
Vie intricate e muri possenti
Che i nostri antenati c'hanno lasciato
Case arroccate, alcune cadenti,
Che il fascino non hanno deturpato.
Esce il turista, ringrazia giocondo
Ha visto il borgo più bello del mondo.

Ferrini's Archway

Legendary archway that invites all
to the village where time has stopped.
Tangled paths and mighty walls
left by our ancestors.
Houses perched, some falling
that do not ruin the charm.
The tourist leaves with thanks, wholly
* cheerful*
He has seen the village of all the world
* most beautiful.*

(Right) Mario reciting his poem L'Arco dei Ferrini

Mario reciting his ode to
the clock tower

Outside the synagogue

From the arch, we proceed along the Via Giovanni Selvi, once the
vibrant commercial center of Sorano. Nowadays, most shops are
shuttered, and Mario remarks about what had been in each: a milk
store, a bar, a general store. We stop in front of the small synagogue
at 20 Via Selvi. Mario recalls that until it was recently recognized
as an important landmark, it was used as a wine bar and then a
fruit and vegetable store for many years. The last shopkeepers –
Superga, a midget, and her sister Alvida – are remembered fondly.
They would fill a wheelbarrow with brined lupini beans and baked
and salted pumpkin seeds and push it up the rather long way to the
playing field outside of town. Soccer matches were very popular
events in the 1960s, unlike today when only a handful of people
attend them. Superga and Alvida would quickly sell out the snacks,
wrapped up in cones
of newspaper.

A few more paces, and
we arrive at the Piazza
della Chiesa, the Church
Square. Here Mario
recites another of his
poems, inspired by the
high clock tower that
watches over the square
and the center of town.

The church square and clock tower

La Torre Dell'orologio

Bel baluardo posto in cima al Masso
con quell'occhione, ciglia e sopracciglia
lor che ti fecer sasso dopo sasso
voller lasciarci questa meraviglia
c'hai visto tutti, passo dopo passo
tutto tu sai, d'ogni tua famiglia.
Per ogni evento il suon non si colora
suoni per tutti prima ed ultim'ora.

The Clock Tower

Beautiful rampart set above the "masso"
with that eye, eyebrows, and eyelashes
those who wrought you stone upon stone
wished to leave us with this wonder
you've seen us all, year after year
and know everything about all your families.
Your sound is changeless for every event
you ring for all the first and the last hour.

Carrying on down the Via Roma, we soon come to a ceramic store established by Beatrice Bandarin, one of those first calamitati drawn by the "magnet" of Sorano. This is where Mario's bar was before he moved to the larger locale. Soon thereafter, we are at the Via dell'Arco, an arched passageway under the church that leads after 20 yards to the beginning of the Via del Ghetto and Antonio's cantina. Used by Antonio and Carlo's father as a smithy, the small forge and a few of his ironworks are still on display. But most impressive is the deep *gola*, the "throat" of the cantina that leads down in the volcanic tufo to chambers that stay at about 10 degrees Centigrade (50 Fahrenheit) throughout the year and are perfect for storing wine. Antonio fills a bottle from one of his barrels, and we enjoy the crisp white wine with the delicious sfratti.

Antonio and Mario head back to the bar, and before I turn to my home across the lane, I look at another plaque on the wall next to

the cantina. Written on it is a poem by Fiorella Bellumori, wife to Adolfo Mezzetti – a close friend, frequent cantina companion of Antonio, and the attacking forward on that same 1960s Sorano soccer team. Fiorella's poem is a powerful memorial to some dark chapters of history.

Il Ghetto	The Ghetto
Il tuo nome non è gloria,	*Your name is not glory*
ma sarà imperituro nella storia,	*but is immortalized in history,*
è urlo che percuote l'universo,	*a cry that smites the universe,*
per evocar il sacrificio inferto	*to invoke the sacrifice inflicted*
a chi ignaro della trama ordita	*on those who, ignorant of the conspiracy woven,*
anelava a vivere la vita.	*yearned to live life.*

Mario wrote another poem inspired by the people who have been drawn to Sorano by the mythical magnet. Entitled "La Calamita," it begins, "In this town it is understood, We are struggling with the magnet. Around the world, if there is someone that is a little strange, By twists and turns he ends up in Sorano." One such down-and-out Italian fellow showed up penniless – "without shoes." He was helped and embraced by the townspeople and ended up creating a business and making a small fortune. He shrewdly bought several properties in town, including where Mario's pastry shop and bar are located. He aggressively raised the rent and then refused to renew Mario's lease. Ironically, Mario, the much-loved maker of sfratti, was essentially evicted and forced to shut down his business. This sad event caused great consternation, but now that some time has passed, I think Mario, at age 76, realizes that he really could not have gone on much longer, sacrificing himself on four hours of sleep a night, seven days a week. He now enjoys sitting on a bench in the piazza, chatting with his pensioner cronies, going for long walks, rediscovering Sorano, and being inspired to write more poetry. But Sorano is poorer for no longer having Mario's excellent pastries and sfratti.

Gli Sfratti

Makes about 10 honey-and-walnut rolls

250 grams (½ pound) honey

Peel of 1 orange, minced

250 grams (2 cups) walnuts, finely chopped

25 grams (2 tablespoons) fine breadcrumbs

500 grams (4 cups) flour

125 grams (⅔ cup) sugar

½ teaspoon bicarbonate of soda

2 eggs

50 milliliters (¼ cup) milk

150 grams (5½ ounces) butter, sliced

Egg whites, whipped

To make the filling, heat the honey in a pot on very low heat for about 15 minutes. Add half of the orange peel and the walnuts to the honey, cooking and continuously stirring for another 10 minutes.

Thoroughly mix in the breadcrumbs and set the mixture aside to cool. In a bowl, sift the flour, mix in the sugar and the bicarbonate of soda, and form the mixture in a pile on your work surface. After making a crater in the middle of the pile, drop in the eggs, two tablespoons of milk, the other minced half of the orange peel, and the sliced butter pieces. Mix, then knead the dough thoroughly, adding a splash or two of milk to keep the dough stiff but elastic. Put the dough in a refrigerator for about 30 minutes.

On the well-floured work surface, take large handfuls of the honey-and-walnut mix, and form them into 15 x 3 centimeter (1¼ inch) cigar shapes. Roll the dough out very thinly to about ¼ centimeter (⅛ inch) thickness, and cut it into approximately 12 x 18 centimeter (7-inch) strips. Place a cigar onto each strip and roll them up in the dough, sealing the ends. Brush the sfratti with whipped egg white and bake them in a 190 degrees C/375 degrees F oven for about 15 minutes, or until the sfratti are nicely browned.

Episode 10
Tastes of Dominica

Episode 10

"Too Many Cooks" by the Dominican band
Windward Caribbean Kulture plays over the credits
to the first I Foodini video from Dominica. WCK
are the progenitors of Bouyon, a well-known music style in the West
Indies. When the episode opens, Jenn Andreoli and I are sitting on a
wall at the Zandoli Inn, with the Grand Bay below us and the town
of Berekua (also known as Grand Bay) in the background. Dominica
is the last refuge in the Caribbean for the native Amerindian
Kalinago people. The original settlement on the Grand Bay was
called Bericoua, which in the Kalinago language means "the place
of large crabs." Land crabs were an important part of their diet, and
stuffed crab backs are still a popular Dominican dish. In the 18th
century, a freed slave from Martinique acquired land on the bay
from the Kalinago and erected a "beautiful" large stone cross that
stands to this day. So, some people have told me, with perhaps a
shorter historical memory, "Berekua" is actually a Dominican creole
corruption of the French words for the cross – Belle Croix.

(Above) I gave the name La Gawenne to the Dominican fruit wines.
In creole it means "rabbit warren."

Jenn and I begin by having the first taste of a batch of grapefruit wine I had made some weeks before. Drawing on my over two decades of experience making wine from grapes in Italy, I was sure I could do the same with the abundance of tropical fruit in Dominica. Some fruit, like grapefruit and mangoes, comes from heritage trees planted on old estates, whereas papaya and passion fruit are harvested from more recently planted private gardens. Much of it sadly goes to waste. The amount of rotting fallen fruit was surprising to me. So, my idea was to buy fruit from the farmers of the Belvedere agricultural cooperative – from which I was also planning to buy some land to create a winery that would benefit the local community of Delices. Jenn's large kitchen, 20 minutes away, proved to be the ideal place to make the experimental batches.

The next scene is of Tariq Baron and Chris Alexander picking grapefruits from Chris's trees in Zion. Rastafarians will often refer to their peaceful and productive country gardens as Zion, which is contrasted to the oppressive and exploitative Babylon of modern municipalities. Tariq is a much sought-after tour guide on the island, and his childhood friend Chris is a farmer who sells his produce at the market in the capital, Roseau. Chris is better known as Ti-Nassief, meaning Little Nassief, as he was named after the Lebanese merchant Elias Nassief who in the 1940s bought the large

Ti Nassif picking and tossing grapefruits to Tariq below. Ti Nassief is also a spin bowler for the Dominica cricket team, but the smoke is not produced by his quick delivery.

Geneva estate to the north and west of Berekua. Nassief was a very successful businessman, and as Chris is a shrewd broker, the name is undoubtedly a moniker of respect. However, Elias proved to be the worst type of denizen of Babylon. His practice of expelling itinerant farmers from his land was so unpopular that around the time of Dominica's independence, he was expelled from the Geneva estate, and his properties were burned to the ground. Subsequent agrarian reform in Dominica meant that some of the largest estates were divided up and distributed to the rural peasantry – not unlike what happened in Italy in the 1950s – so Ti-Nassief got his little plot carved out of the Geneva plantation.

Collecting sorrel hibiscus with Lucille at the Belvedere Estate

I then go to another farmer's field in Delices and collect cultivated sorrel hibiscus calyces. Once the *Hibiscus sabdariffa* flower falls, the bright red sepals expand and become an accessory fruit used to make a thirst-quenching drink in the West Indies. My thought was that it would add a nice color and complementary flavor to the grapefruit juice. Back in Jenn's kitchen, Tariq hand-squeezes the freshly picked grapefruits as I boil the hibiscus fruit in sugarcane juice that I had pressed in Roseau. The addition of the resultant red syrup was necessary to increase the sugar content of the fruit juice so that, once fermented, the wine would contain about 13% alcohol – ideal for preservation. The first batch of grapefruit wine was lovely but quite tart. The next time I made it, I added papaya juice, an alkaline fruit that reduced the acidity, and the result was perfect – an excellent light rosé. The other wine I produced was a mango and passion fruit mix featured in one of the later 1 Foodini live-streamed pilot videos for Nom.com. Restaurateurs and hoteliers around

Black Chris and White Chris preparing the mango and passion fruit juice

the island highly appreciated both wines, and I was planning to ramp up production significantly. Unfortunately, later that year, Dominica was blindsided by Tropical Storm Erika, which in some places dumped an astounding 11 inches of rain in an hour and resulted in total accumulations of as much as 33 inches. There were massive landslides, many lives were lost, much of the town of Petite Savanne was swept into the sea, and the essential eastern coastal road that connected Stowe, where the Zandoli Inn is located, and Delices was destroyed – and has never been reopened. The trip from the Zandoli Inn to Delices, which once took 20 minutes, now takes an hour and a half. The Inn was filled with mud, and my winemaking plans were shelved. Then, only two years later, Dominica was devastated by Hurricane Maria.

(Below) Fermenting mango and passion fruit juice

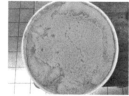

Chris overseeing by Skype from Italy the first racking of the mango wine in Dominica. Jenn and Tariq say it is delicious and goes very well with the baked crab backs

Scotty and wild yam

Scotty high up in a centuries old
mango tree

Following the winemaking scenes, we are introduced to my very
good friend Scott Lewis, aka Ambush. Scotty is a Rastafarian who
has renounced material trappings and lives a very simple life deep
in the bush with his menagerie of goats, dogs, and chickens. I met
him when I was hacking my way with my machete through the area
of Belvedere, near Delices, where he makes his home. We quickly
determined that we were born on the same day of the same year,
which sealed our fraternal bond, and he has been my close adviser,
guide, assistant, and generally a very helpful Man Friday ever since.
He has introduced me to many local people, has been my go-to guy
for much of the fruit, fish, and other things I have needed, and we
have been on some wonderful expeditions together.

On this occasion, we go fishing. My idea was to go to the White
River in Delices, which I had heard has a lot of large, particularly
tasty crayfish. I also saw it as an opportunity to visit Victoria Falls,
one of Dominica's most impressive waterfalls. The source of the
falls and river is the Boiling Lake, which is the largest fumarole in
the Western Hemisphere. We begin by hiking up to the base of the
falls, and it was not an easy climb through brush and over boulders.
The falls are very high and feathery – not at all like what I was
expecting – but we then make our way back down, swimming in
pools and catching quite a lot of crayfish. As we leave the area, we

stop off to visit another Rastaman by the name of Moses James, aka Wed, who has created a lovely garden and guest house on the banks of the White River at a place he calls Zion Valley. When I described the falls Scotty and I had been to, he was surprised. He revealed that we had not been fishing on the White River, nor had we gone to Victoria Falls. Rather we had gone to Jack Falls, also known as Angel Falls. Moses said, cocking his head at Scotty, that locals also call it Tough Falls because getting there is so tough. Scotty looked sheepish but explained smilingly that the Jack River was better for crayfish.

Scotty below Jack Falls

Back at the Zandoli Inn, I prepare spaghetti with shrimp because the crayfish were just out of season when the segment was recorded. This simple dish proved to be a hit when I was cooking at the Inn, as was the dessert, a sweet avocado parfait that Joana, my baba – nanny – made me when I was a child in Salvador, Brazil. I used the magnificent large avocados from a massive tree on the hotel property. When they were in season, I had to compete with Rockette, one of the hotel dogs, to get them. Once they fell from the tree, she would gobble them down to the extent that she would become quite rotund. Unfortunately, Hurricane Maria knocked down that towering avocado tree. Jenn serves the spaghetti and parfait to two friends, Celeste and Elise, in the Zandoli Inn dining room.

(Left) Joana, me, and my mother in Brazil. (Right) Dressed up for Salvador Carnaval.

(Left) Dressed up for Roseau Carnival (Right) Asa Bantan at carnival.

The video then returns to the day when Scotty and I hiked to Tough Falls. As Scotty dances with a hooked crayfish, we cut to a crowd dancing during Carnival. Asa Bantan, the famous Bouyon singer from Berekua, is on top of a truck stacked with blaring speakers and pushes the dancers forward through the streets of Roseau.

My companion for the Carnival festivities has become another excellent friend. Henry Shillingford is a Rastafarian lawyer brought up partly in Queens, New York. He was, when still young, a very successful entrepreneur. Henry rubbed shoulders with people in the music industry and made his mark managing musicians and producing albums. He was, for example, the executive producer of *True Democracy* by Steel Pulse. He soon determined that he could best help his musician friends by providing them with legal

representation, and so went on to get a law degree in London. Upon returning to Dominica, he changed course and became involved in environmental causes. He was instrumental in preventing a copper mine from destroying a vast area of Dominica's pristine Central Forest, for which his associate and close friend, Atherton Martin, won a Green Nobel – the Goldman Prize. Henry represented Dominica worldwide at International Whaling Commission meetings and UN and NGO conferences on the environment and sustainable development. By the time I met him, his days of environmental activism were a fading memory. Still, he occasionally takes on controversial causes, supports underdogs, and maintains his reputation as a good troublemaker. I was introduced to Henry by Jenn from the Zandoli Inn. I then engaged him as my real-estate lawyer, and subsequently we became business associates in a renewable energy concern.

Henry with his daughter Leslassa. She was carnival queen that year- and went on to represent Dominica at the Miss World contest

On the day of the unofficial opening of Carnival, J'ouvert, I collected Henry before daybreak at his delightful old wooden Shillingford estate house at Snug Corner, which sadly was also to be destroyed by Erika, and we drove on to Roseau. I wore one of Jenn's mother's nighties, as I was told that was a popular Carnival attire for men, and Henry dressed up in a kaftan and headscarf. We partied until the late afternoon and returned another day for the continuing Carnival celebrations. I then made my way late in the night from Roseau to Delices and hooked up with Tariq and Ti-Nassief – who also plays horn for a Grand Bay traditional Carnival Lapo Kabwit ("goatskin" in creole) drum band. We smoked and drank and danced until dawn.

Spaghetti with Shrimp
(or Prawns or Crayfish)

4 servings

500 grams (1 pound) shrimp, topped, shelled and deveined
4 tablespoons olive oil
5 garlic cloves, chopped
150 ml (⅔ cup) white wine
5 tablespoons butter
Dash of hot sauce
Salt and pepper to taste
500 grams (1 pound) spaghetti

Put a large pot of salted water to boil. Fry the shrimp in a large hot skillet with the oil. Once the shrimp are pink and cooked through, after about 4 minutes, remove them from the pan, leaving the oil with the shrimp essence. Add the garlic and a sprinkle of salt to the pan, and let it cook for a minute or so until the garlic is soft. Pour in the wine, and let it reduce for a couple of minutes.

Meanwhile, put the spaghetti in the boiling water. Melt the butter in the pan on low heat. Add a dash of hot sauce. Put the shrimp back in the pan and toss them in the buttery garlic sauce. Reserve ⅓ cup of the pasta water and drain the al dente spaghetti in a colander. Add the spaghetti to the pan with the pasta water and mix. Give a good grind of black pepper and serve immediately.

Creme De Abacate *(Avocado parfait)*

4 servings

1 large or 2 medium ripe avocados
⅓ cup powdered sugar
5 tablespoons lime juice
½ cup whipping cream

Peel the avocados and cut them into pieces. Place in a blender with the sugar and lime juice. Cover and blend until smooth and creamy. Put the blended avocado in a bowl. Fold in the whipped cream.

Serve chilled in parfait glasses.

Come to Dominica

De Elf

Episode 11
Lobster Risotto

Rockette and Scratches at
Woches Cassées

Episode 11

Vincent Cyril Henderson, aka De Elf or just Elfie, is a talented artist
and musician to whom Jenn Andreoli introduced me. I have since
visited him many times at his home and gallery on the Lalay – the
main drag of Berekua – and collect his fantastic artwork. Elfie
originally played bass in the 1970s for a Berekua band called Black
Machine and then walked across the Lalay and joined the very
successful Midnight Groovers for 15 years, touring Europe, the
United States, and Canada. I asked him to create a theme song for
the Dominica edition of I Foodini that would "big up" Dominica
and the Zandoli Inn. He wrote the sweet tune "Come to Dominica,"
and we made a simple music video. The song highlights the
characters, places, and elements of the second Dominican video.
The first two verses are "Come to Dominica, Check out the
Zandoli Hotel and then have a good time, a great time in sunshine.
Come to Dominica, Check out Foodini and the crew, and to
eat some lobster, lobster ya ya in sunshine, sunshine. Come to
Dominica, Check out Mr. Ambush, and you will get the great fruit
wine, great fruit wine in sunshine, sunshine." The main dish I
prepare is a lobster risotto, and Jenn makes a delicious grapefruit
wine sangria, among other things.

Dominica is the youngest of the volcanic islands in the Caribbean, and the Valley of Desolation and the Boiling Lake are reminders of its continuing activity. The video opens at Point Carib, jutting into the Atlantic, at the furthest extent of the hotel property. Jenn and I are actually at a place that is locally known in creole as Wòch Kasé, or broken rock, where magma flowed into the sea recently enough that it remains craggy and bare. Jenn begins by speaking of the history of the place. It is where Jeannet Rolle – the freed slave who made a business pact with the Kalinago people at Bericoua – arrived, but also where escaped slaves from the plantations in Martinique landed and then made camps in the densely forested interior of the island. These Maroons later became a force to be reckoned with by British colonists. I speak of the geology of Wòch Kasé and point out that, with its nooks and crannies, it created an ideal habitat for rock lobsters.

Jenn and her son Wynton at Woches Cassées

I then go north along the coast, eight kilometers as the crow flies but about 16 kilometers as my car drives, on the very windy and steep road from the Inn at Point Carib to the entrance of the trail to Glasse Point – another very beautiful place where an even bigger flow created a lava field beside the ocean. I collect Mathias Regis (aka Dready) and Scotty and his two dogs Whitey and Blackjaw, at Delices on the way. Dready was shot and had his leg amputated during a sad chapter in Dominica's relatively recent history. Rastafarianism was introduced to the island in the early 1970s and was quickly demonized. The Catholic majority and government officials viewed the Rastafarians' countercultural, socialist, and Afrocentric views, back-to-nature ethic, and use of cannabis as so threatening that in 1974 Dominica's parliament passed the Dread Act, which suspended due process for people wearing their hair in dreadlocks. Rastafarians were arrested without a warrant and were not permitted bail. At best, they were forced to submit to the indignity of having their dreads cut. Civilians and the police were granted immunity from prosecution for harming Rastafarians, so many were assaulted and killed. Scotty had his arm shattered when he, too, was shot by the police. He escaped from his guarded hospital room and recovered hidden in the rainforest, treating an infection and the poorly set break with natural remedies. Moses from the previous chapter was also shot and still walks with a bad

Scotty and goats. Because he can scramble just about anywhere I call him kabwit montany- mountain goat in creole

Dready does not mind that I call him Pelican

limp. Even Henry Shillingford, a lawyer from a respected family, not long ago was arrested by the police on a trumped-up charge of marijuana possession. He was beaten and had his leg broken. The Dread Act was finally repealed in 1981. In those seven years, at least 21 Rastafarians were murdered.

As I spent two years on crutches, I greatly appreciate Dready's skills. I have been on a few hikes with him, and he can get up and down slippery rainforest slopes on his crutches faster than most bipeds. He does not disappoint as he bounds down the track to the ocean. There we meet Scotty's son Dickson and his cousin Jathelle, who are assigned the task of getting me rock lobsters. Scotty, who trained Dickson to fish, and Dready also jump into the ocean to do their own fishing.

Pelican takes flight

After about an hour, the older men emerge from the turbulent water with their catch, and we make our way back to the car. We go on to Delices, where Scotty quickly sells his fish, and we stop off at Alec's bar, where we have a few games of dominoes – one of Dominica's most popular pastimes. Meanwhile, Dickson and Jathelle have been snorkeling for five hours along some seven kilometers of coastline, and we meet up with them at a rocky beach below Delices – with many more lobsters than I needed. But the word spreads, several locals come, and they quickly sell out.

Back at the Zandoli Inn, Jenn and I set about cleaning and boiling the lobsters. I then make a lobster risotto, and Jen prepares a baked macaroni and cheese pie. Mac and cheese is commonly served in Dominica on weekends and at family celebrations, but Jenn has tweaked the standard recipe, and it became a staple dish at her restaurant in Toronto. As I noted earlier, Jenn is also an excellent mixologist and makes one of the best rum punches I have ever had. This time she makes a fantastic sangria with my grapefruit wine.

That afternoon, Tariq comes with his sisters Tahnee and Wendy and Wendy's children. Ti-Nassief and Elfie also stop by, and we sit down in the garden and have a feast with the risotto and mac and cheese, all washed down with the grapefruit wine sangria.

Lobster Risotto

6 servings

1 kilo (2.2 pounds) lobster meat
3 liters (3 quarts) boiling water
1 large onion
6 garlic cloves
6 small carrots
3 celery sticks
1 bay leaf
lobster shells
2 tablespoons olive oil
1 medium-sized onion, finely chopped
750 grams (3⅔ cups) arborio risotto rice
150 ml (⅔ cup) white wine
30 grams (3 tablespoons) butter
85 grams (3 ounces) Parmesan cheese
Salt and pepper to taste

I bought about 20 small rock lobsters from Dickson, and the tails provide the meat in the Caribbean, but obviously, lobsters from northern climes with claws can equally be used. Jenn and I cleaned and tailed the lobsters and then boiled them for about four minutes. The meat was extracted, and some shells were reserved for the broth.

To make the broth, I put on a large pot of water and bring it to a boil with the onion, garlic, carrots, celery, and bay leaf. It simmers for about 2 hours. The lobster shells are added for the last half hour (they can make the broth bitter if they are in for any longer). I pass the cooked broth through a colander into another smaller pot, and then press the vegetables through a medium-fine sieve, adding the vegetable puree that results to the clear broth.

I put the olive oil and onion into a wide, heavy-bottomed pan and gently fry until soft. I stir in the rice so that the grains become very lightly toasted and coated with the oil, and then pour in the glass of wine and continue to stir until absorbed. I add a ladle of the hot broth and turn the heat down to a simmer. While continuously stirring the rice, I gradually add the broth a ladle at a time until it is all absorbed. Once cooked, in about 15 minutes, the rice is creamy and slightly firm. I remove it from the heat and stir in the butter, grated Parmesan cheese, and ⅔ of the lobster meat. Salt and pepper to taste. The reserved pieces of lobster are used to garnish the individual plates.

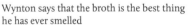
Wynton says that the broth is the best thing he has ever smelled

Jenn's Mac and Cheese

6 servings

250 grams (9 ounces) mozzarella
250 grams (9 ounces) sharp Cheddar cheese
3½ tablespoons butter
4 scallions, chopped
1 handful chives, chopped
1 handful parsley, chopped
1 celery stick, chopped
5 seasoning peppers, chopped
½ green pepper, chopped
½ teaspoon nutmeg, freshly grated
1 teaspoon of pepper
2 pinches of salt
¼ cup white flour
½ cup white wine
4 cups milk
Splash of hot sauce
1 tablespoon butter
2 tablespoons cassava flour
1 kilo (2.2 pounds) short pasta
2½ tablespoons Parmesan cheese

Jenn begins by grating the mozzarella and Cheddar and then makes a green béchamel sauce. In a pot, she melts the butter and then adds the chopped scallions, chives, parsley, and celery for the green seasoning. Jenn notes that green seasoning is very commonly used in West Indian dishes. It includes a variety of green garden vegetables and seasoning peppers, which are scotch bonnets that are sweet – not hot. She grates the nutmeg into the pot and adds the ground pepper and salt. Then a third of a cup of the flour is stirred in, followed by the wine and the milk. After a dash of hot sauce, she lets the sauce thicken by slowly coming up to boil.

Jenn butters a large 35 x 23 centimeter (14 x 9 inch) Pyrex lasagna dish and evenly distributes cassava (tapioca) flour – made by a neighbor – to create a nonstick surface. She empties the bag of pasta into a pot of boiling salted water, and while it is cooking, she adds and melts most of the grated mozzarella and Cheddar into the green béchamel sauce. Jenn reserves a handful of cheese to make a streusel-type crunchy topping for the dish. She drains the pasta one minute before the total cook time, puts it into a large bowl, pours on the cheesy béchamel sauce, and mixes. Jenn spoons the pasta into the Pyrex dish. She hand-mixes the butter, cassava flour, and Parmesan cheese for the topping and sprinkles it over the top of the mac and cheese. The oven was pre-heated to 200 degrees C/390 degrees F, and Jenn puts the dish in for about 15 minutes, or until the top is golden brown.

Jenn's White Wine Sangria

1 medium-sized pineapple
90 milliliters (3 ounces) sugar syrup
1 bottle of white wine
60 milliliters (2 ounces) triple sec
160 milliliters (5.5 ounces) rum
Splash of angostura bitters
500 milliliters (17 ounces) Sprite
330 milliliters (11 ounces) club soda

Jenn deconstructs the pineapple. She efficiently tops and tails it
– reserving the top to plant in the garden. She slices off the peel,
which she uses to flavor a simple syrup: she adds the peel to equal
parts sugar and water, which she boils for about 10 minutes. Jenn
cuts the pineapple into small cubes and puts them in the freezer. In
a large jug, she pours in a bottle of my grapefruit wine – although
a good dry pinot blanc or sauvignon blanc would also work well –
and also the sugar syrup, triple sec, rum, Sprite, and soda. When it
is ready to be served, she adds the pineapple cubes.

Tahnee says that the lobster and rice was the best she had ever had

Episode 12

*Prosciutto wrapped
dorado with
cush-cush gnocchi*

Episode 12

The third and last Dominica episode begins with Jenn and me chatting on the terrace of the Zandoli Inn. Jenn explains how she came to live in Dominica and speaks of her experience as a chef in Canada, running her own restaurant, and then returning to Dominica and eventually fully taking over the hotel's running from her mother. We move to the kitchen, and I begin the day's meal preparation by making the *primo piatto*. The "first plate" in Italy is generally made with pasta, but on this occasion, I make gnocchi – Italian dumplings, usually made with potato.

In Dominica and all of the English-speaking West Indies, "ground provision" is the term for the tubers and roots that people tend to eat every day, much like rice in Asia and pasta and bread in Italy. The commonly used ground provisions have many different names, as most were imported as seeds from throughout the world. In Dominica, there are sweet potatoes (*Ipomoea batatus*), but also cassava (*Manihot esculenta*), taro (*Colocasia esculenta*), and tannia (*Xanthosoma sagittifolium*). Generally, they are boiled and served with meat or vegetable stews or salted fish. My favorite, cush-cush

(*Dioscorea trifida*), is a yam indigenous to South America that was brought to Dominica by the Amerindians more than a thousand years ago.

In the Zandoli Inn kitchen, I always tried to incorporate locally available food, like crayfish, rock lobster, and avocado. This time I use cush-cush. I found that the consistency of the yam is much like a potato, but the flavor is sweeter and the lavender color quite fantastic. Mashed cush-cush makes the best gnocchi I have ever had, and I think the few people who have tasted them would agree.

After making the cush-cush gnocchi, we cut to the local fishery at Fond St. Jean. We are there when the fishermen come in with their day's catch. I buy two dowad, as the fish is locally known. In other parts of the world, it is called dorade, dolphin fish (not to be confused with the mammal), and mahi-mahi. The dowad is filleted by one of the fishermen, and Jenn cuts the fish into individual portions to be served to the hotel guests that night.

Back at the hotel, Jenn makes one of her signature dishes, baked dowad, wrapped in prosciutto with her take on a chimichurri sauce

– using what is available from her vegetable garden. She then makes a delicious chocolate pudding, using chocolate made by a woman down the road from her own fermented and roasted cacao seeds.

Jenn sets a table on the terrace for her son Wynton Gabriel and her step-daughter Sydney. They are our guests for the meal of gnocchi and dowad. Later in the afternoon, Kerlin, the accountant, comes for work and gets the reward of one of the chocolate puddings.

The episode closes with a quick visit to Scotty in Delices. He shows us some cacao pods that the seeds are extracted from, and an old cast-iron cauldron used at one time for roasting the seeds on the plantation. It is now full of water and used for watering cattle – and Scotty thinks it is an excellent time to give Whitey and Blackjaw a bath.

Cush-Cush Gnocchi with Butter and Sage

6 servings

1 kilo (2.2 pounds) cush-cush
200 grams (7 ounces) white flour, plus plenty for dusting
130 grams (4½ ounces) butter
16 medium-sized fresh sage leaves, chopped
¾ cup of grated Parmesan cheese

My favorite potato for gnocchi is the Yukon Gold variety, but I was delighted to discover that using the cush-cush yam may be even better. Scrub the tubers well, and steam them for 20–30 minutes, or until tender. Allow to cool. Gently peel or strip off the skins, as the lovely purple color is contained within the thin cortex of the tuber, whereas the central pith is white. Mash with a fork to a smooth consistency without lumps.

Liberally dust your work surface with flour, and mix and knead the cush-cush and flour together to form a smooth dough. Take a handful of dough at a time and roll out using your fingers to form

rolls 2 centimeters (¾ inch) thick. Cut into pieces 3 centimeters (1¼ inches) long. Continue in this way until all the dough is finished.

Pick up a dumpling at a time, and with the tines of a well-floured fork, make an indentation on one side. Leave to rest on a clean cloth, occasionally dusting with flour, so that if the individual gnocchi come into contact with each other, they don't stick.

Melt the butter in a pan, add the chopped sage leaves, and cook on low heat for 4 minutes.

Prepare a large pot of salted water and bring it to a boil. Add the gnocchi in three batches, cooking each separately. When the gnocchi rise to the surface of the boiling water – about 1–2 minutes – they are cooked. Lift out with a slotted spoon and layer them in a serving dish. Each batch is drizzled with three tablespoons of the butter and sage. Continue until all the gnocchi have been used. Serve immediately with grated Parmesan cheese.

Prosciutto-Wrapped Mahi-Mahi

6 servings

900 grams (2 pounds) mahi-mahi filet
6 thin slices of prosciutto
Green seasoning (see Jenn's Mac and Cheese, page 94, for recipe)
For Jenn's Chimichurri Sauce:
1/2 handful cilantro, lightly chopped
8 leaves mint, lightly chopped
8 leaves Thai basil, lightly chopped
1handful of parsley, lightly chopped
1 sprig of thyme
2 sweet potato leaves, chopped
1 clove garlic, peeled and chopped
zest from ½ lime
2 pinches salt
4 tablespoons olive oil
For the garnish:
2 carrots, sliced
pink peppercorns

Jenn takes 150-gram (5-ounce) flat portions of the mahi-mahi filet, smears them with a teaspoon of green seasoning, and sprinkles each with a pinch of salt. She rolls the fish first because she likes the prosciutto to stay on the outside, then rolls each fish roll in a slice of prosciutto. In a hot pan, she places the rolls seam side down, to make sure the rolls stay together, then turns them so the prosciutto is browned on all sides. She places the pan in a 190 degrees C (375 degrees F) oven for 5 minutes. For a garnish, Jenn quickly roasts two sliced carrots in a pan.

For the chimichurri sauce, Jenn explains that she is using what is available from her raised bed garden. At the time, she did not have oregano and other herbs available, so in place of cilantro, for example, she uses what is known in Dominica as chadon beni (also called Mexican coriander). She also uses a tropical broadleaf thyme, *Coleus aromaticus*, of the same genus as the popular ornamental plant and known by many names – Cuban oregano, Mexican mint, or Indian borage. She lightly chops up the various green herbs and vegetables and garlic clove, places them in a bowl with the lime zest and olive oil, and blends with a hand blender until smooth.

For the kids' lunch, and then again later in the evening for the hotel guests' dinner, Jen decoratively applies two tablespoons of the dark green chimichurri sauce to the plates. She adds to each plate 10 of the purple gnocchi, which I made simply with butter this time as the sauce is so flavorful. Jenn cuts the rolls in half, places two pieces on each plate, and garnishes with the carrot slices and pink peppercorns – quite a feast, if just for the eyes. Not only that, because Jenn's son Wynton proclaims that the meal is "bursting with flavor."

Jenn's Cacao Faux Mousse

6 servings

3 tablespoons butter
3 tablespoons sweetened condensed milk
200 grams (7 ounces) dark chocolate
Pinch of salt
30 milliliters (1 ounce) local rum
30 milliliters (1 ounce) triple sec
3 pinches mixed spice
225 grams (8 ounces) cream cheese

Jenn creates a double boiler by putting a large metal bowl over a pot of boiling water. In the bowl, she melts and whisks together the butter, condensed milk, and chocolate, to which she adds the salt, rum, and triple sec. Because she uses cacao, which is locally made chocolate with spices, the recipe also calls for mixed spice powder.

One time when Jenn was planning to make a chocolate mousse for dessert and did not have cream, she used cream cheese instead. She was very pleasantly surprised by the result and so called it her "faux mousse."

Once it is melted, she transfers the warm boozy, buttery chocolate and sweet milk mixture to a food processor and pulses it first with half the cream cheese and then again with the second half. When it is blended and smooth, Jenn serves the cacao mousse in espresso cups.

Episode 13

Pizza with
Gianfranco

Episode 13

Not much of a better way to return to Italy than with this next installment of I Foodini, as Sean and I go to a pizza party. Aurelio Fierro sings "A Pizza," which the credits open to, about a simpler time, or perhaps quite simply a uniquely Italian and highly improbable fantasy of buying love with pizza. He meets a girl with cherry-red lips and smelling like roses, and he wants to give her a 14-carat diamond, but all she wants is a pizza topped with tomato sauce. He would take her to the finest restaurants, but again all she wanted was a pizza margherita. He even manages to marry her, and when the five-tier cake comes, all she desires is the simplest of pizzas and nothing else! If only... There is little doubt that a pizza in Naples is one of life's great culinary experiences, but with a good wood-burning oven and the best ingredients, an excellent pizza can be made anywhere. On this occasion, we visit with Gianfranco and Ada Franci to celebrate their daughter Luisa's birthday. Luisa is the companion of Nicola, the proprietor of the Ottava Rima, featured in episode 6.

There had been more than one year's hiatus from the previous video made in Italy. As we once more drive the Citroën – this time from Sorano to the eight-kilometer-distant town of Pitigliano – Willie Nelson's "On the Road Again" comes to mind for some reason. Remarkably Sean, too, remembers the lyrics, and so we, perhaps unfortunately, provide our abbreviated rendition. As we arrive at a bend in the road, we see the dramatic view of Pitigliano.

I note that there has been a centuries-long rivalry between Sorano and Pitigliano. To learn more about that, we cut back to Sorano and Mario Lupi, the baker/poet we met in the last Italian episode.

I walk with Mario in Sorano's old town again, from the medieval entrance along the Via Roma. Just before the small church square, we stop at a plinth with a large cannonball placed on top, and Mario reads his poem "La Storia dell'Orso" ("The Legend of the Bear"). Mario relates in rhyme the story of a group of men from Pitigliano who, in the 16th century, decided "over a flask of wine" to hijack the travertine marble bear – a symbol of the then ruling Orsini family – from Sorano. They were led by a fellow named Collofino, "a rascal, perhaps even more so than a fox, who pulled off stunts, but always avoided the blame." Arriving in the dead of night, they made off

with the bear and put in its place a lopsided cannonball (a further insult) which is now known as the "bear's ball." They concealed the bear in a *giubba* – a cloak – and from that time, the people of Pitigliano are commonly known as the "Giubbonai."

We return to Pitigliano, where it just so happens that Luisa's birthday this year coincides with the movable feast day of Corpus Domini, known as the Feast of the Most Holy Body and Blood of Christ – a celebration of the Eucharist. In Pitigliano, the two main streets of the old town are carpeted with flowers. We first meet Luisa, as she, like many of the townspeople, is involved with gathering the flowers and making the sometimes quite intricate designs. The biggest and most elaborate pattern is in front of the impressive 13th-century Cathedral of Saints Peter and Paul. At the far end of the square is a 20-foot column, and on top of that is the hijacked bear from Sorano.

The first three stanzas of Mario Lupi's "The Legend of the Bear":

Ero in città... a Pitigliano
camminavo lungo il corso
mani in tasca, distratto e piano piano
mi trovai al Duomo
proprio davanti all'Orso.

I was in town... in Pitigliano
walking along the way
hands in pockets, distracted. Finally
I found myself at the cathedral
right in front of the Bear.

Salute mi sento dire... o Capacciolo!
qual bon vento ti porta a 'sto paese?
Sto sopra a 'sto palchetto tutto solo
e gioisco quando vedo un soranese.

"Salutations," I heard... "Capacciolo!*
What good wind brought you here?
I am up on this column all by myself
and joyous to see you from Sorano."

Mi avvicino ancora a quel palchetto
gli dico! Ma tu parli il mio dialetto!
M'hanno messo qui sopra ma da tanto
ma io so' soranese e ME NE VANTO.

I approached the column,
saying to him, "But, you speak my dialect!"
"They put me up here a long time ago,
but I am from Sorano, and PROUD OF IT."

*The nickname for people from Sorano is Capaccioli, meaning "hard heads," as they are a notoriously stubborn bunch. The name likely comes from the fact that Sorano was under siege many times from the Sienese over 40 years in the 15th century and the townspeople had countless cannon and catapult balls rained upon their heads, one of which is on my mantle – and another is the large one that substituted for the bear in the church square.

Sean and I move on to Nicola's garden, where we are greeted by the birthday girl and her parents, Gianfranco and Ada, and her uncle Valerio. Valerio is busy making a delicious *moscardini in guazzetto*, musky octopi in a tomato sauce, which is one of several

additional dishes on offer for the party. A *sugo alla poverella* was made by Gianfranco to go with the pasta. The surprising range of ingredients included prosciutto ham, mushrooms, olives, and tuna, and my remark was that with all that, it was hardly a "poor man's sauce." I did not have the courage to try it, but I was told it was very good. Our primary interest is Gianfranco's pizza, and so we move on to the wood-fired oven that is well on its way to reaching a temperature of about 400 C/750 F. A table is set up to stretch and flatten the pizza dough, but first Ada demonstrates how to mix the flour, yeast, oil, and water. As the dough needs a couple of hours to rise, another batch of dough was pre-prepared, and that is rolled into individual balls and brought out from the kitchen. Ada and her granddaughter Benedetta prepare the pizza discs, and Gianfranco slides them into the oven to cook. And so we learn Gianfranco's secret: he pre-bakes the pizza bases so that when he puts on the simple toppings of tomato sauce and grated mozzarella, the base

stays crispy. He then puts the pizzas back in the oven to finish the cooking. The result would undoubtedly have turned Aurelio Fierro's wife's head. One of the best pizzas I have had outside of Naples.

The pizzas keep coming, and the gathered two dozen folks contend with the other ample offerings, including roasted pork and countless bottles of Gianfranco's decent white wine. As is printed in Italian on his wine labels, "When you are happy, drink to party. When you are sad, drink to forget. When you have no reason to be happy or sad, drink to make things happen." As suggested, much drinking is done, and once we finish the wine, the liquor cabinet is raided. We have some good grappa, but some other wonders emerge – vodka made in Trieste and Jamaican rum made in Padua. Somehow Sean, I, and the Citroën make it back to Sorano. As the closing credits play, Willie Nelson sings "On the Road Again."

Gianfranco and Mario's Peace Pizza

Makes 10 pizzas
For the dough:
3½ teaspoons sugar
14 grams (5 teaspoons) active dry
   yeast or 42 grams (1½ ounces)
   fresh yeast 500 milliliters (1 pint)
   tepid water
1 kilo (2.2 pounds) white bread flour
3½ teaspoons salt

180 milliliters (¾ cup) olive oil
For the topping:
800 grams (28 ounces) good-quality
   peeled Italian tomatoes
2 teaspoons salt
3 tablespoons oregano
750 grams (26 ounces) mozzarella
Drizzle of extra virgin olive oil

As I have lived in Sorano for the better part of the last 30 years, I have eaten more pizzas there than anywhere else. The main reason is that Mario Lupi, the poet of "The Legend of the Bear" and the baker of sfratti of the ninth episode, would invite friends and family to his bar on most Sunday evenings for pizza. Mario's pizza is also one of the best I have ever eaten, but it is different in one particular respect from Gianfranco's – and it is Mario's secret. He says, *"nella pizza mai risparmiare olio"* – with pizza, do not spare the oil. In fact, his recipe calls for using 180 milliliters (¾ cup) of olive oil, which is far more than in Gianfranco's recipe. Mario believes that the oil makes the crust crunchier and more digestible.

The Latin *restaurare*, to repair or renew, is the root of "restaurant," indicating the healing nature of a good meal. So, in the spirit of comity, and to symbolically pacify the rivalry between the two towns, I have combined the two recipes of Pitigliano and Sorano, and the result is optimal.

Mix the sugar and yeast in the water and let sit for five minutes. In a bowl, mix the flour and salt. Pile the salted flour onto your work surface and make a well. Pour the yeasty water and oil into the well. Using a fork, in a circular motion, incorporate the flour into the well until the dough begins to bind. With floured hands, knead the dough for a couple of minutes. As Ada Franci says, the dough should be worked as little as possible, just until it is smooth, elastic, and no longer tacky. Place the dough in a bowl dusted with flour. Cover with a tea towel and leave for 2 hours.

Once risen, make 150 gram (5.3 ounce) balls of the dough. On a flour-dusted surface, roll out the dough into approximately 25 centimeter (10 inch) rounds that will nicely fit a dinner plate. Set aside the discs of dough to rise for another half hour. As Gianfranco's oven is wood burning, the temperature can get as high as 400 degrees C/750 degrees F, so the pizzas cook very quickly. In a conventional kitchen oven, the temperature should be 250 degrees C/475 degrees F. When the oven is up to temperature, the pizza rounds can be cooked for 8 minutes on greased pizza trays or baking pans.

To prepare the pizza topping, put the peeled tomatoes, salt, and oregano in a bowl and mix with a hand blender until the tomatoes are broken up and the sauce relatively smooth. The pre-cooked pizzas can be covered with the tomato sauce using a medium-sized ladle. Roughly tear 75 grams (2½ ounces) of mozzarella onto each pizza, give a good drizzle of olive oil, and put the pizzas – ideally two at a time – back in the oven for another 8- 10 minutes, or until the mozzarella has melted and the borders of the pizzas are browned.

"Pizza restored," thanks to the commingling of the recipes from Pitigliano and Sorano. Now to make full amends, all Pitigliano has to do is return the Orsini bear to its rightful place in the church square of Sorano.

Episode 14

Eggplant Parmigiana

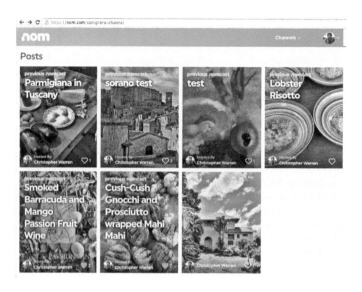

Episode 14

The inimitable Mina accompanies the opening credits. Her song "Ma Che Bontà" is very well suited to the dish that Sean and I prepare, *una parmigiana di melanzane*, an eggplant casserole.

Cosa c'è nella padella	What's in the pan?
Mmm che profumino	Mmm, that smells good
Fai assaggiare un pezzettino?	Let me taste a little bit?
Ma che bontà, ma che bontà	But how delicious, how delicious
Ma che cos'è questa robina qua	But what is this stuff here?
Ma che bontà, ma che bontà	But how delicious, how delicious

The first parmigiana I ever tasted was cooked by my friend Maurizio Mezzetti. I distinctly remember walking into his home and remarking about the wonderful smell emanating from his oven. If I had not been told the ingredients, I might have been hard-pressed to identify the baked amalgamation of fried eggplant, tomato sauce, garlic, basil, mozzarella, and Parmesan cheese. It was delicious!

This might not have been a 1 Foodini presentation if there had not been a total communication breakdown when Sean and I attempted to make our first Nom.com webcast from Sorano. I introduce the episode by explaining that I had already done other webcasts for Nom, from Dominica and Manhattan, with varying degrees of success. In the first live show, when Jenn and I were asked to reproduce the purple gnocchi and prosciutto-wrapped mahi-mahi, the Nom platform was still in beta. The web connection was poor and the image choppy, which was a disappointment. The second webcast was about Jenn's smoked barracuda and my mango/passion fruit wine – which go very well together. The connection was good and the show very much appreciated. I was then asked to do my lobster risotto with friends in Manhattan. The webcast began at the appointed time – or so I thought. Only when I had cooked the meal, and we had raised our glasses, was I contacted by the technicians in Los Angeles – why had I not begun the show? None of it had been broadcast. So the parmigiana in Sorano was my last stab at a live Nom cooking show. Because it takes almost two hours to prepare and cook the dish, Sean and I made one of the casseroles in advance, and I took still pictures of each step of the process and presented them in slide format as we were cooking another casserole live. There were further technical problems, and the show again was not broadcast – and Nom closed shop entirely not long afterwards. Doing live cooking webcasts was a good idea, but their technicians were not up to it.

So Sean and I and friends enjoyed the two parmigiana casseroles we had made, along with several liters of my wine and an impressive amount of grappa. The next morning I blearily thought that we could make good use of the still photographs I had taken. I called Sean and invited him over to help me narrate the making of a parmigiana while flipping through the photos – intercut with filmed segments of us sitting at my kitchen table drinking some strong cups of coffee. So, that is the unconventional but effective form that this episode takes. Mina has the last word, while the closing credits pass: "Ma che bontà, ma che bontà!"

Parmigiana

6 servings

3 large eggplants, cut into 1
  centimeter (⅜ inch) slices
3 garlic cloves, peeled and roughly
  chopped
Olive oil
800 grams (28 ounces) peeled plum
  tomatoes
Salt and pepper
500 milliliters (1 pint) sunflower oil

2 beaten eggs
½ glass water
White flour
2 handfuls fresh basil leaves
300 grams (10.5 ounces) buffalo
  mozzarella
10 tablespoons grated Parmesan
  cheese

Sprinkle both sides of each eggplant slice with fine salt, lay the
slices out flat on a work surface, and leave to sweat the bitter liquid
for about twenty minutes. Gently cook the garlic in 1 tablespoon of
olive oil until soft. Add the tomatoes, season with salt and pepper,
and simmer for 15 minutes. Now rinse the eggplant slices and
pat dry. Heat the sunflower oil in a frying pan. Beat the eggs and
water together. Dust each eggplant slice with flour, dip into the egg
mixture, and fry in the oil until golden on both sides. Remove the
slices and allow to dry on kitchen paper.

Cover the bottom of a deep ovenproof dish with some of the
eggplant slices. Pour ¼ of the tomato mixture over the slices. Tear
up four basil leaves and shred ⅓ of the mozzarella, and scatter on
top of the tomato sauce with a generous sprinkle of the grated
Parmesan and a drizzle of the olive oil. Repeat the layers until all of
the ingredients have been used up, finishing the top with the last
of the tomato sauce and more Parmesan. Place the dish in a 180
degrees C/350 degrees F oven and cook for about 30 minutes or
until golden.

Episode 15

Breadmaking &
Olive Oil with
Katrina & Martino

Episode 15

This last episode begins where we ended the previous show – back in my kitchen. But this time I'm alone, as Sean is off helping Katrin and Martin, who were introduced in the third episode, harvest their olives. I start by making sourdough bread. A few years ago Vincenzo Rizzuto, from the eighth episode, gave me the wonderful gift of a *lievito madre*, a sourdough starter that he says had been used uninterrupted in his family for 200 years. He demonstrated to me how to make bread by this traditional method using natural leavening, which has been eschewed by most modern bakers who now use faster-working chemical yeasts to make their bread rise. One of the reasons I was eager to bake my own bread was that the town baker had recently closed up shop, so there was no local bread available anymore. Also, quite frankly, I do not much like Tuscan bread, which is made with white processed flour and no salt. It is tasteless and goes stale after just one day.

As holding a camera and kneading bread are mutually exclusive, I decided to break my rule of primarily recording with my iPad. A friend lent me his GoPro camera, which I mount on a tripod and then on my head to show my vantage point as I make the dough. Bread was the staple food in old Sorano and all of Italy, to the

extent that everything eaten with a portion of bread (*pane*), was called *companatico* – the bread accompaniment. As a brief aside, and further indicating how essential bread was to European society, the word "companion" also derives from the Latin *companio*. *Com* means "with," and the second part of the word is the Latin word for bread. A companion is someone with whom one breaks bread.

On this day, I make two loaves of bread. The companatico for the first loaf is bratwurst sausages that Katrin and Martin brought from Freiburg in Germany for the olive harvest lunch. The second loaf's companatico is the freshly pressed olive oil that we taste later in the evening at the local wine bar – the Cantina dei Sapori.

Once the bread is baked, I put the GoPro on my cycling helmet and jump on my mountain bike, rather than driving in the Citroën, to go the two kilometers to the olive grove. There we see the harvest in action. After three days, a total of 2,000 kilos of olives is picked from the 150 trees. Those olives are then placed in stackable crates

and transported to a *frantoio* – an olive oil mill – in Pitigliano. At the mill, we see the mostly automated process of cleaning the olives of leaves and other impurities. The olives are crushed into a paste and then pressed to extract the oil. Martin and Katrin return to Sorano with 300 liters of extra virgin olive oil – a respectable yield of about 15 percent oil per weight of olives.

This harvest is in October, a generally busy time for musicians, but Martin and Katherine's orchestra provides them with a special dispensation because so many of their colleagues are very happy to get the excellent olive oil they produce. If they did as the old people from Sorano and waited until even as late as January to harvest the olives – and some still do – they could get well over a 20 percent yield. Olive oil is not a luxury in Italy. It is used in almost every meal, so locals tend to be more impressed with quantity than

quality. But with greater maturity comes much more acidity, so the quality is lessened considerably.

The olive picking crew all join up again at the Cantina dei Sapori to enjoy a few bottles of wine and taste the delicious new olive oil. Later that night, some of us gather for an impromptu concert played by Oliver Erlich, Martin, and Katrin. Excerpts from two pieces they play – the Sonata for two cellos in G major by Jean-Baptiste Barrière and the Duet for cellos in D major by Franz Joseph Haydn – are used for the opening credits, while I am cycling up to the olive grove, and for the closing credits.

In small towns in Italy bread was traditionally of the sourdough variety. The culture used to make the bread rise is derived from a mixture of flour and water that ferments due to the interaction of naturally occurring wild yeast. Essentially invisible micro-organisms, *Saccharomyces cerevisiae*, help foodies create magic out of thin air, whether it be by fermenting wine or bread. So it seems appropriate that the last recipe in this book should be about the magic of bread making.

It takes a few days, but it is relatively simple to create a sourdough starter. In a medium-sized glass or ceramic bowl, combine a quarter cup of rye flour and a quarter cup of warm tap water. If the weather is warm, the bowl can be covered with a cloth and left at room temperature for 24 hours. If it is cooler than 20 degrees C/68 degrees F, the bowl can be left in the oven with the oven light on to give minimal heat. The next day, add another quarter cup of flour and a quarter cup of warm water and let sit for another 24 hours. This is repeated on the third day. On day 4, remove half of the mixture and discard it. To the remaining mixture, again add a quarter cup of flour and a quarter cup of warm water. The mixture should be bubbly and have a sweet aroma by the fifth day. If not, continue to add a quarter cup of flour and water each day. By day 7, the mixture will certainly be alive and doubling in size. It is ready to be used as a starter. I keep about a large fistful of the starter in a mason jar in the refrigerator and generally make bread once a week. If the starter is not used within seven days, it needs to be replenished by discarding half and adding half a cup of flour and a quarter cup of water and mixing.

In the years I have been making bread, I have over time come up with my preferred mix of flour: an equal combination of rye, verna (an old Tuscan grain variety), farro ("emmer" in English, and now a well-known ancient grain), and regular white bread flour. In the video, I make two loaves of bread, but here I provide the measures for making one 1.3 kilo (3 pound) loaf.

200 grams (7 ounces) rye flour
200 grams (7 ounces) verna flour
200 grams (7 ounces) farro flour
200 grams (7 ounces) white bread flour
12 grams (½ ounce) salt
1 large fistful of sourdough starter
475 milliliters (1 pint) warm tap water

Mix the flour, salt, and starter in a large plastic or ceramic bowl. Add the warm water and mix with a plastic spatula. Once the water is absorbed, continue to mix in the bowl with floured hands. Flour

a wooden board and use the spatula to scrape out all of the dough from the bowl. Knead the bread for about 3 minutes. If the dough is still very tacky, add a little flour and continue to knead until the dough is elastic and very slightly sticky. Put the ball of dough back in the bowl, and if the room is warm – above 20 degrees C/68 degrees F – then cover with a tea towel and leave for 4 hours. If the room is cold, put the covered bowl in the oven, and turn on the oven light. One can also put the oven on for 30 seconds to warm it before putting in the bowl. After 4 hours, the dough has risen and needs to be "punched down" or flattened with floured fingers on the work surface. Take a large fistful of the dough and place it in the glass mason jar and back in the refrigerator – that is the starter for the next week's bread. The remaining dough is then rolled up into a loaf form, enveloped in a floured tea towel, and put, seam side up, into a Pyrex dish, and left again to rise. After 2 hours, the dough is ready to be put into a 230 degrees C/450 degrees F oven. Turn the dough out of the dish and place it on a baking tray that is covered by a thoroughly wetted and squeezed-out piece of parchment paper. I cut two shallow slits in the top of the loaf and then leave it to bake for 55 minutes. I have a ventilated oven, so I turn the fan on for the first 35 minutes of baking. After 35 minutes, turn off the fan and turn down the oven to 180 degrees C/350 degrees F for the last 20 minutes of baking.

Afterword

Over the course of 20 videos and webcasts, some considerable culinary magic is imparted by I Foodini – we pass along the secrets of wonderful dishes from Italy to Dominica. It has now been two years since the last show, and the three *maghi* ("magicians" in Italian) have parted company. In that time, I published *Feasts from Paradiso*, which was the expressed aim of the first video, and now have finished the work of this book. Sean, who escaped London and the demanding job of being a chef to move to Italy and pursue other ventures, has now come full circle. At the beginning of 2022, he will become the proprietor of the wine bar and restaurant where we first met 15 years ago – the Cantina dei Sapori. Jenn is living in Hamilton, Canada, with her son Wynton. The three disasters of Tropical Storm Erika, Hurricane Maria, and the coronavirus pandemic devastated tourism on Dominica, and Jenn had to leave the island just to survive. The Zandoli Inn is being cared for by my friend Henry Shillingford and awaits the return of Jenn or the arrival of someone new. Perhaps in time, the three of us, Jenn, Sean, and I, will meet and finally all together create more I Foodini magic in my kitchen in Sorano or Jenn's restaurant in Dominica.

Thanks go to all the Foodini who made this book possible.